# THE
# ILLUSTRATED ENCYCLOPEDIA
# OF ANIMAL LIFE

## THE ANIMAL KINGDOM

The strange and wonderful ways of
mammals, birds, reptiles, fishes and
insects. A new and authentic natural
history of the wildlife of the world.

### FREDERICK DRIMMER, M.A.
#### EDITOR-IN-CHIEF

George G. Goodwin
*Associate Curator of Mammals,*
*The American Museum of Natural History*

Charles M. Bogert
*Curator of Amphibians and Reptiles,*
*The American Museum of Natural History*

John C. Pallister
*Research Associate, Insects,*
*The American Museum of Natural History*

Dean Amadon · E. Thomas Gilliard
*Associate Curators of Birds,*
*The American Museum of Natural History*

Christopher W. Coates *Curator*
James W. Atz *Assistant Curator,*
*Aquarium of The New York Zoological Society*

## VOLUME 9

GREYSTONE PRESS, NEW YORK

**The Common Trumpeter** is blackish with long, bright-green legs and a short green bill. Its tail is stumpy and soft, and the feathers about the neck are short and velvety with deep, iridescent, purplish reflections. The brilliant effect is enhanced by the vivid tan on the lower back and wing feathers; the inner flight feathers are elongated and grayish.

This bird feeds in large flocks on fallen fruit gathered in the depths of the tropical forest. When an intruder happens to come upon such a flock, the trumpeters fly noisily into low perches nearby and gawk at him. If he is a hunter he will have no trouble wiping out most of the group. Since trumpeters are very tasty eating, they soon become scarce or disappear altogether when man makes his appearance.

In Brazil, however, the trumpeter is often domesticated and allowed to associate with barnyard fowl. It is reported to make an excellent "watchdog," calling noisily at the first sign of danger at night. Though the trumpeter is a friendly, charming pet, it apparently will not breed away from its home grounds.

## BUSTARDS—AMONG THE HEAVIEST OF FLYING BIRDS

There are some twenty-three species of bustards, all of them Old World birds. They are medium sized to large, related to the cranes, but with shorter legs and heavier bodies. Bustards are partial to dry plains and run swiftly. On the steppes of Asia they are often hunted on horseback. Some of the larger bustards weigh thirty pounds or more, and are among the heaviest of flying birds.

Bustards have an exceptionally varied diet, eating seeds, green shoots, insects, small reptiles, and even mice or birds. Their flesh is considered a delicacy. They lay two to four protectively colored eggs in a shallow, unlined depression on the ground. Africa is the stronghold of this family (the Otididae), but several species are native to Asia and one to Australia.

**The Great Bustard,** *Otis tarda,* was killed off in Britain as early as 1838. However, it is still found in Poland and elsewhere in eastern Europe and parts of Asia. The great bustard's over-all color is gray, with black wing quills. It has long white bristles at the base of the bill, while other kinds of bustards are ornamented with a variety of bristles or plumes, which they display in the courtship postures or dances. The male has a gular (throat) pouch of thin skin. At pairing time he struts around with the throat pouch inflated, head thrown back against the shoulders, tail erect and spread and wings drooping. Very quarrelsome at this season, the males utter threatening booming sounds, probably produced by the sudden expulsion of air from the throat.

## SUN BITTERNS AND THEIR EXTRAORDINARY DANCE

**The Sun Bittern,** *Eurypyga helias,* is found only in the tropical parts of the New World. It is related not to the bittern, as we might expect, but to the crane tribe, and makes up a family by itself, the Eurypygidae. The sun bittern is remarkable for a dance performance that is quite out of the ordinary, as it spreads its wings and tail in a nearly horizontal horseshoe which, umbrella-like, completely hides its body. The wings of this bird have broad maroon centers, black, gray, and white tips, and broad, yellowish olive bases. The amazing dance displays this brilliant wing pattern to best advantage.

The sun bittern has a slender neck and head, the latter being black with a white stripe under the eye. The throat and abdomen are white, the upper parts gray barred with black. Together with the wing pattern already described, this adds up to a very striking color scheme.

Sun bitterns feed on insects and small fish. They place the nest of sticks, grass, and mud in a tree in flooded river-bottom forest. The eggs are reddish buff with black markings.

## KAGUS—FLIGHTLESS BIRDS OF NEW CALEDONIA

**The Kagu,** *Rhynochetos jubatus,* dwells only on the large island of New Caledonia, some thousand miles east of Australia. This bird, which figures on the postage stamps of New Caledonia, is about the size of a chicken and is the sole member of the family Rhynochetidae. It has gray plumage, to which the orange-red of its feet is a vivid contrast. The wing quills are boldly barred with white, and the kagu displays them at courting time in much the same remarkable manner as the distantly related sun bittern of tropical America. Barely able to fly, the kagu is active chiefly at night. Formerly there were no predatory mammals on New Caledonia; but now that cats, dogs, pigs, and rats have been introduced and much of the forest cut off, this strange bird faces extinction.

**STRANGE BIRD OF THE SOUTH SEAS**

An ancient, almost flightless bird, the kagu lives only on the Pacific island of New Caledonia. Noted for its remarkable courtship dance displays, the kagu is mainly active at night, and feeds on worms and slugs; by day it hides among rocks or the roots of trees. Kagus engage in amusing antics and often erect their tall crests.

## CARIAMAS—ANCIENT AND DIGNIFIED

The cariama is still another of the ancient types of cranelike birds. There are two species, both natives of South America and members of the family Cariamidae; both are stately, long-legged birds with long tails and a bustard-like mane of hairy feathers growing from the crown and neck. They are notable for their erect posture and their preference for spending most of their time on the ground. These qualities remind us of the secretary bird of Africa—though naturalists usually consider that bird to be more closely related to the eagles than to cariamas or cranes.

**The Gray Cariama,** *Chunga burmeisteri,* dwells in northern Argentina. Including its tail, the bird is about three feet long. Above, it is smoky brown sprinkled delicately with buff and becoming gray with profuse black bars on the head and mane. There is white around the eye and on the abdomen. The throat, neck, and chest are colored like the head but with **finer black barring. The wings and tail have heavy gray and white bars.**

We find cariamas in grassy semiwooded regions, sometimes in flocks, more frequently in pairs. The nest, constructed of twigs, is placed on the ground or in a bush or low tree. The cariama lays two pale eggs with brown markings. We are told that the cariama's call resembles a dog's bark!

**THE CARIAMA PREFERS TO STAY ON THE GROUND**

A stately, long-legged bird which spends most of its time on the ground, the cariama, of South America, has a long tail and a mane of hairy feathers. Berries and insects are prominent on the cariama's menu, but it will also eat snakes and lizards.

### THE DIATRYMA—FANTASTIC FOSSIL

There is a possibility that the giant fossil running birds discovered in the Eocene rocks of North America may be related to the cariama. These primitive birds must have been extraordinary creatures, judging from the largest and only complete example, *Diatryma steini*, now on exhibit in the American Museum of Natural History in New York City. Standing more than six feet tall, the relic is equipped with a tremendous skull and a bill of the general shape of a meat cleaver, though somewhat larger.

### FINFEET—SKILLFUL SWIMMERS, SLUGGISH FLIERS

Finfeet are curious grebelike water birds of tropical South America, Africa, and Asia. They have the bill of a rail, lobed feet, short legs, elongated bodies, and long, pointed wings. There are only three species, all of them belonging to the family Heliornithidae. Very secretive birds, they take to the water to hide. They dwell in swamps and wooded streams, building a crude nest in a mass of vegetation a few feet above the water. Though finfeet run, swim, and dive with great ease, they are heavy and sluggish when it comes to flying. They sprint furiously with the lobed feet in taking flight.

**THE FINFOOT—STRANGE BIRD OF THE TROPICS**
The finfoot (or sun grebe) is a strange tropical bird with fascinating ways. Thoroughly at home in the water, it does not care much for flying. This bird lives along sluggish streams and dives as skillfully as the true grebes. It places its nest in tangled vegetation a few feet above the water. The New World finfoot, above, has lobed, banded feet, as shown.

The New World Finfoot, *Heliornis fulica,* is dull olive with a blackish head, neck, and tail. White stripes decorate the sides of the head and neck. The bill is reddish and the feet are curiously banded with black and yellow.

## BUTTON QUAILS—DRUDGERY IS FOR MALES

All sixteen species of the button quails live in the warmer regions of the Old World. Ranging from five to seven inches long, they look like miniature quails. In every case the female is larger and more brilliantly colored than the male. She flouts tradition in other ways as well, for it is she who attracts a mate by booming courtship calls, and it is the male who shoulders the duties of incubation and bringing up the young. After the female has laid a clutch of eggs and left them for her mate to incubate, she is believed to repeat this procedure with a second mate.

The nest, located in a grassy depression in the ground, is sometimes domed with grass. A clutch consists of three to five cone-shaped, spotted eggs. Covered with down when they hatch, the young are able to run as soon as they leave the shell. Button quails feed on insect larvae, berries, and seeds. These ground-dwelling birds, also known as hemipodes or bustard-quails, are related to the rails, and compose the family Turnicidae.

When we observed button quails in the Philippines and New Guinea, they confirmed their reputation for being exceedingly shy and often difficult to flush from the tall grass where they live. They run strongly, but when sufficiently startled they flutter for short distances over the grass and then drop abruptly into it.

The Collared Hemipode, *Pedionomus*, of Australia, differs from the other members of the Turnicidae in several ways and is often placed in a separate family.

## RAILS, COOTS, AND GALLINULES

The 132 species of this worldwide family are running birds with long legs and toes and a slender body for slipping through dense vegetation—so slender, indeed, as to give rise to the phrase, "thin as a rail." Most of them live in marshes or swamps, though many tropical rails dwell in forest areas. As for the lobe-toed coots, they swim and dive as expertly as ducks. Rails usually have a mottled or spotted plumage pattern of brown, yellow, chestnut or other modest colors. However, some of the gallinules and swamp hens are bright purple.

Most rails have a varied repertoire of loud notes—sometimes eerie whistles, other times henlike cackles. Often their voices have a ventriloquial quality that deceives a listener if he tries to locate the birds. Many years ago an unknown bird, dubbed "the kicker" because its call sounded like *kick-kick-kick,* was heard in marshes along the Concord River in Massachusetts by a goodly number of expert bird-students. All efforts to get a glimpse of the bird failed, but it was probably the Black Rail, one of the sparrow-sized and characteristically shy members of the family.

Rails are excellent game birds—they are delicious eating and, despite their mediocre flying abilities, are exceptionally elusive. The approved hunting technique is to pole about the marshes at high tide. This forces the Sora and Clapper Rails to fly rather than to run when approached by a boat. Then they offer the gunner a good target.

Rails, as you have gathered, are very secretive, running through the dense grass with great swiftness when disturbed and resorting to flight only when they have no choice. Though they have small wings, many of them make lengthy migrations at night, and the family is well represented on remote islands in all parts of the world. Several of the island species have completely lost the power of flying.

The members of this family, known as the Rallidae, feed on insects, tubers, seeds, worms, water plants, mollusks, and occasionally lizards and mice. Here are some typical American representatives of the family:

**The Clapper Rail,** *Rallus longirostris,* which makes its home in salt marshes, is a brown bird half the size of a chicken. It has an unfortunate habit of flying low on migrations, and is therefore prone to flying accidents. Like many rails, it engages in dances, performed to the accompaniment of a crescendo of screeching notes. The clapper rail fashions its nest of grasses and places it on the ground in salt marshes. The young—and this is true of most rails—are black and very precocious, being able to swim and run almost as soon as they are hatched.

**The Purple Gallinule,** *Porphyrula martinica,* is a brightly colored species which dwells in the warmer parts of the New World. About eleven inches long, it swims well and favors ponds choked with water plants. It flies more readily than most rails and is easily identified on the wing. A crimson bill, bluish forehead shield, and conspicuous under-tail quills set off its purple plumage. The purple gallinule's nest is a platform of reeds in cane grass and rushes. The four to ten eggs are white with reddish markings.

**The American Coot,** *Fulica americana,* ranges from Alaska to Ecuador. About the same size as the clapper rail, it has longer wings and sometimes flies in great flocks. It feeds mostly on vegetable matter. Related species dwell on the other continents. They are all slaty-gray birds, usually with a conspicuous, white, chicken-like bill.

## SOME OTHER RAILS AND THEIR ELUSIVE WAYS

As we have seen, rails are fond of wet terrain. Still, some species, such as the Wood Rail, *Rallina eurizonoides,* live on the floor of deep tropical jungle that is relatively dry. Others—the large, sooty-gray Grass Rail, *Rallus torquatus,* for example—often visit fields some distance away from water. This makes it difficult for us to generalize about where rails prefer to live.

Many kinds of rails live on tiny, bleak, sometimes arid islands far out on the ocean. The flightless Wake Island Rail, *Rallus wakensis,* had only one reasonably permanent source of drinking water: the tiny caches of rain water that collect in mollusk shells! Other kinds of rails live out their lives within hailing distance of their birthplace. This is forcibly brought home to us by the Iceland Rail, *Rallus aquaticus,* which dwells in tiny oases surrounding hot springs.

Then there are rails so strongly concentrated in a local area that they become "lost." Take, for example, the large flightless rail, *No-*

**NOTORNIS—LOST AND FOUND**
Flightless birds concentrated in a remote area can easily become "lost" to science. That is what happened to *Notornis,* a member of the rail family. From 1900 on, it was considered extinct. Yet half a century later naturalists discovered this bird dwelling on the shores of a mountain lake in New Zealand.

*tornis hochstetteri,* which in 1949 was discovered in some numbers in New Zealand living along the shores of an alpine lake. Yet the experts had considered the bird extinct for half a century! Other kinds of rails, which are known to us from only a few individuals, are really very common. We had an instance of this kind in the case of the Schomburgk Rail, *Micropygia schomburgkii,* a starling-sized brown and yellow denizen of the highland grass fields lying between the Amazon and Orinoco Rivers. One day in 1938 our Indians started a grass fire and casually trapped more than twenty of these birds. Before that, hundreds of hours of hunting in the same fields, both by natives and white men, had yielded only a single example of this "rare" bird.

# Shore Birds, Gulls, and Their Relatives

Most of the birds grouped in this order, such as the sandpipers, plovers, and gulls, live on the water or near it; a few dwell on arid plains. Naturalists divide the shore birds proper into ten families—the best known are the sandpipers and the plovers. Most shore birds have long legs—their feet are not webbed—and are swift runners. The bill is adapted for picking small insects and other food from mud or shallow water. These birds almost invariably place their eggs on the ground. The young are cute little balls of down; they run after their parents almost as soon as they are hatched. Among several families of shore birds we note a trend toward reversing the usual nesting behavior of birds. Among these families the female is more brightly colored and assumes the initiative in courtship; so we are not so surprised to learn that it is the male who incubates the eggs and cares for the young.

The pratincoles, a group of Old World shore birds, are

long-winged, short-legged birds which feed on insects they catch on the wing as swallows do. We may think of them as forming something of a transition to the other main division of this order—the gulls and terns. These birds, unlike the shore birds, have webbed feet. They live near salt or fresh water. The young, though born with down, are less active than those of shore birds and usually linger near the nest for some time after hatching.

The relatives of the gulls include the jaegers and the skuas—aggressive and almost hawklike, they often catch and eat small birds and mammals. The strange lily-trotters or jaçanas—birds with unusually long toes adapted for running over water plants—present a problem to naturalists. Usually the experts place them with the shore birds, though there is a theory in some quarters that the lily-trotters may

**THE POMARINE JAEGER—ARCTIC HUNTER**

The German word for "hunter" is Jaeger—an appropriate name for this large gray and black marauder which hunts for lemmings and small birds on its Arctic nesting grounds. It spends the winter at sea in latitudes as far south as central Africa and even Australia. The jaeger keeps well offshore and we rarely see it in the United States.

be more closely related to the rails. The auks and puffins are also believed to be related to the shore birds and gulls. The birds described in this chapter make up the order Charadriiformes.

## SANDPIPERS—BIRDS OF THE SEASHORE

You can readily see how the sandpiper got its name—it lives, with a few exceptions, on sandy beaches and has a piping cry. The sandpiper family (the Scolopacidae), with seventy-seven species, is the largest group of shore birds. Most members of the family breed in the Far North and winter along southern seashores. Their long legs are useful when it comes to wading in mud or shallow water. Still another adaptation for life on the beach is their long bill, which they use to pick small crabs or insects from the ground or mud. Despite the absence of bright colors, shore birds are attractive, alert birds, with varied plumage of brown, gray, white, or chestnut. They place the four rather large, pointed eggs in the nest with the small ends together. In this way the eggs form a circle that the incubating bird is just able to cover. The nest is not an impressive affair—a mere depression in the grass or sand, sometimes sparingly lined with grass.

**The Woodcock,** *Philohela minor.* This is the New World species of one of the few sandpipers that do not visit the shore. It is a plump, big-headed, brown bird, about twelve inches long. Its unusual appear-

### THE WOODCOCK—POPULAR GAME BIRD
Nicknamed the "timber-doodle," the woodcock has a long probing bill which enables it to drill for earthworms far below the surface of the mud. The tip of the beak is flexible, and can be opened underground to seize the prey. Even while intent on its meal, the woodcock can see approaching enemies, for its eyes are placed high on its head.

ance has won for it such names as "Timber-doodle." It does much of its feeding by probing with its long bill in mud for earthworms. The woodcock can open the soft, sensitive tips of this bill to seize a worm far below the surface of the mud. You might think that the bird is in an exceedingly vulnerable position when its bill is buried deep in the mud; but the woodcock's eyes are placed rather high on its head, enabling it to see an approaching enemy.

During the spring, woodcocks assemble on courtship grounds. The male utters sharp *peent*-like notes and then rises high in the air and circles about. He descends in a series of dives, meanwhile delivering beautiful twittering notes. While we do not know for certain, there is some reason to believe that this music is produced by the air rushing through the narrow, stiff outer wing feathers, rather than by the vocal cords. The woodcock is one of the most popular game birds.

**The Jacksnipe or Wilson Snipe,** *Gallinago delicata,* was given its scientific name because it is a table delicacy. Less than twelve inches long, it is related to the woodcock, and performs in much the same way during courtship. The snipe's notes, which have a bleating quality, are produced by the air rushing through the stiffened outer tail feathers. In the case of the Pintail Snipe of the Old World, we find that all of its tail feathers are almost as stiff and slender as toothpicks.

While the woodcock prefers alder bogs, the snipe frequents open marshes or wet meadows. Both have rather solitary habits and are distributed throughout the United States. Consequently they have not been so seriously reduced by hunting as the other American shore birds, and are still on the list of game birds. All sandpipers are strong fliers, the snipe especially so, which makes it a very difficult target for the sportsman.

**The Spotted Sandpiper,** *Actitis macularia,* is a small bird—about eight inches long. To the country boy it is the "Tip-up" because of its habit of teetering back and forth as it sits nervously on a sand bar or log. The spotted sandpiper can run rapidly when necessary. Found almost throughout the length and breadth of North America, it is most common near water, though it will occasionally live in dry fields. The newly hatched young, like all baby sandpipers, are covered with soft down. Their colors blend perfectly with their surroundings. Before migrating south in the fall, the spotted sandpiper loses its spots and becomes plain white below. We observe this molt into a simpler winter dress among most sandpipers.

The many kinds of sandpipers that are at home at the seashore range in size all the way from the tiny Least Sandpiper, a bird scarcely larger than a sparrow, to the curlews and godwits, which stand about a foot tall. Most sandpipers nest in the Arctic. In the spring they are among the last migrants to go north, lingering in large numbers until late May. When it comes to journeying south in the fall, they are among the first birds to leave, appearing in some numbers on the coasts of the United States as early as July.

Though many sandpipers visit the coasts of the Southern Hemisphere, it is quite unusual for any of them to nest in tropical or southern latitudes. One exception is the little Polynesian Sandpiper, *Aechmorhynchus*, found on the tiny coral islands of the Tuamotu chain near Pitcairn Island in the Pacific. The chances are that it is descended from wandering migrants of some northern species.

As we have seen, many sandpipers breed in the remote north, which has made it difficult for naturalists to study their nesting habits. It took until 1948 to find the nest of the Bristle-thighed Curlew, *Numenius tahitiensis*, an American species that nests on a bleak stretch of tundra in Alaska. When it feels the approach of the arctic cold, this curlew flies more than two thousand miles to Hawaii and other nearby islands to spend the winter. It was one of Captain Cook's famous expeditions that discovered the bristle-thighed curlew on Tahiti, and named it *tahitiensis*.

## PLOVERS—EXTRAORDINARY MIGRATORS

To Europeans the plover is the "rain bird" because of its habit of scolding before rain. ("Plover" is derived from *pluvia*, the Latin word for "rain.") We find the sixty-three species of this family—plovers, turnstones, and surfbirds—in almost all parts of the world. A good many of these birds are famous for their remarkable migratory journeys. Closely related to the sandpipers, the members of the plover family (the Charadriidae) have shorter legs and a shorter bill.

For the most part, plovers are small or medium-sized birds with coloring that runs to quiet hues. They are equally at home on coasts, plains, or fields. All have a relatively large head and a body that is plump because of the highly developed flying muscles. These plump birds are good to eat. In plovers the hind toe is either lacking or very small.

Almost without exception, plovers lay four relatively large eggs in slight depressions in sand or earth. These eggs are cone-shaped and speckled or blotched with brown and black. In Europe, plovers' eggs are eaten a good deal.

**The Golden Plover,** *Pluvialis dominica,* is one of the most outstanding of all migrating birds. About eleven inches long and with a wing spread of some twenty-three inches, it is a good-looking bird, mainly black with golden yellow flecking on the back when it is in breeding plumage. It nests during the short Arctic summer on the tundras of the Far North. With the coming of warmer weather, the snow on these wastes has melted faster than the ground can absorb it, leaving vast marshes that abound in mosquitoes and gnats. The plover snaps these up as well as other insects and worms.

**A FAMOUS MIGRATORY BIRD**
The golden plover nests on the Alaskan tundra in summertime, and with the approach of cold weather makes a nonstop flight of twenty-four hundred miles to Hawaii. In late spring it returns to Alaska. The Atlantic variety of this bird makes a similar nonstop flight from Nova Scotia to South America.

In September, as they sense the long Arctic night coming on, the plovers leave on their nonstop migratory flights. The Pacific birds travel some twenty-four hundred miles, nonstop, from Alaska to Hawaii. Unable to swim well, they make the trip without food or drink or rest, at a speed variously estimated from forty to seventy miles an hour. Thousands take part in this migration, and by April or May they are on their way back to the Far North.

Their Atlantic cousins make a slightly longer nonstop flight from Nova Scotia to the coast of South America, winding up by wintering on the pampas. In the spring these plovers return by a totally different route, navigating north along the coast of South and Central America and then up the Mississippi valley. Yet they return, miraculously, to their ancestral breeding grounds—to nest sometimes at precisely the same spot as before. Old World plovers are noted for similar migrations between the northern latitudes and islands in the Indian Ocean as well as Australia and New Zealand.

**The Killdeer Plover,** *Charadrius vociferus,* gets its curious name from its frantic cry of "Kill-dee." This call is as familiar to farm boys as its broken-wing ruse—a device used by all plovers to draw interlopers away from their nest. After the spotted sandpiper, the killdeer is probably the most common of American "shore birds." It may winter or migrate along the shore, but when the nesting season arrives, the killdeer will spend much of its time on gravelly, sandy, or grassy fields, sometimes close to human habitations. We have found the killdeer nesting, for example, on lawns and football fields. Some ten inches long, the killdeer is a tawny-rumped bird with brown upper parts, white under parts, and two black bands across the breast.

**The Ruddy Turnstone,** *Arenaria interpres,* about nine inches long, is another remarkable migrator. Nesting in the Arctic regions, it travels in the fall to southern Brazil and Chile and sometimes even as far as the Antarctic! You are probably curious about its name, which comes from its unusual eating habits. With its strong bill, this bird turns over stones, shells, and pebbles in search of small crustaceans, slugs, and worms. It also feasts on grasshoppers. A link between the plover and sandpipers, this handsome bird is brilliant reddish brown above, white below, with black markings on the face, chest, wings, and tail.

## OTHER PLOVERS

Of the thirteen plovers we may observe in North America, four are wanderers from foreign shores. One of these, the European Lapwing, *Vanellus vanellus,* can be immediately recognized by its streaming black crest. It was this bird that made one of the most notable flights in the annals of birdlore in 1927, flying twenty-two hundred miles across the Atlantic to Labrador. The lapwings were driven by powerful wind currents and of course did not purposely set out for America! This was the year in which Lindbergh made his famous nonstop flight from New York to Paris, negotiating thirty-six hundred miles in thirty-three hours.

Some Old World plovers are colorfully adorned with accessory plumes. Of these, the most extraordinary is the large Wattled Plover, *Lobibyx,* of Australia—it sports a fleshy yellow masklike wattle which hides the base of its bill and the front of its head. The red legs and wing spurs are also striking in appearance.

Coming back to American plovers, we find the Surfbird, *Aphriza virgata,* on the Pacific coast. It has gray plumage, flies swiftly, and seems to enjoy standing where it is showered by spray from the surf. Its nest remained undiscovered for a long time, but naturalists finally found it high on the slopes of Mt. McKinley in Alaska. On Atlantic beaches we may often see the pale, sand-colored Piping Plover, *Charadrius melodus,* or hear its mournful whistle.

## AVOCETS AND STILTS—LONG-LEGGED WADERS

The avocets and stilts make up a small group of shore birds that frequent warmer regions than those preferred by most true sandpipers. The family is known as the Recurvirostridae.

**The American Avocet,** *Recurvirostra americana,* has a long bill which, as its scientific name informs us, is curved upward. It is plentiful around the alkali lakes of western North America. Up to twenty inches long, the avocet is a large, handsome shore bird with very long legs adapted for wading. Its plumage is varied with white, tan, and buff. The male and female take turns incubating—as one of a pair daintily picks its way over the alkali flats towards the nest, its mate will rise from the eggs and depart. To see this, however, you must be well concealed, for the avocet is very noisy and aggressive when humans approach its nest.

East of the Mississippi, hunters wiped out the avocet, which was once considered a good game bird.

**The Black-necked Stilt,** *Himantopus mexicanus,* is aptly named, for no other bird has such disproportionately long legs. The stilt spends much of its time wading in shallow water, for which its dangling, almost grotesque legs are well adapted. As if the legs needed anything to make them more noticeable, their red color contrasts vividly with

### TAKE-OFF, LANDING, OR JUST RUNNING?

American coots, having longer and stronger wings, fly better than the related rails and gallinules and also can dive rapidly, but when frightened, they skitter across the water like a "skipped" stone, using both their wings and feet to propel them at a good pace. These slaty-gray marsh-dwelling birds with their conspicuous white, chicken-like bill, range the Western Hemisphere from Alaska to Ecuador, and have close relatives on other continents.

### A LAUGHING GULL IN FLIGHT

Many gulls acquire darker plumage on the head and flight feathers during the nesting season, but the precisely outlined black head of the shrill-voiced laughing gull is a permanent, identifying characteristic. One of the smaller gulls, this noisy gabbler flies with the easy grace and strength typical of the family.

L. G. Kesteloo—Va. Comm. of Game and Inland Fisheries

**A LAUGHING GULL AT ITS NEST**

This laughing gull has returned to its nest in a marsh to find one of its eggs broken. Like all gulls, it is willing to make known its displeasure by loud scolding. Sometimes the cries of a large flock of these gulls sound like discordant laughter, whence their name. This bird is common along the coast from New York to Florida and westward on the Gulf Coast.

this bird's plumage—black above, white below. The stilt is about thirteen inches long, the legs about seven inches.

Stilts often nest in the company of avocets in the western United States, and they also dwell in the Southeast. The stilt has close relations in the warmer parts of the Old World. During World War II many American servicemen got their first view of the Hawaiian Stilt, a common bird on the mud flats near Pearl Harbor.

THE AVOCET'S REMARKABLE BILL
Many birds have a long bill, but the avocet's is remarkable because it curves upward. This good-looking bird has very long legs suitable for wading. Avocet parents take turns incubating their eggs, and raise a din if their nest is approached. The avocet is often found in the company of its relative the stilt—a bird that, in proportion to size, has the longest legs of any known bird.

## PRATINCOLES AND COURSERS

The most remarkable bird in this group is a courser—the Crocodile Bird, *Pluvianus*, which—so we are told—enters the gaping mouth of the Nile crocodile in search of leeches.

There are twenty-three species in this Old World family (the Glareolidae), which is partial to the warmer regions. The Common Pratincole ("meadow inhabitant"), *Glareola pratincola,* is perhaps the best known of these birds. It has long, pointed wings, a forked tail, and

weak feet. In flying, it uses the swallow's technique of catching insects on the wing. The common pratincole nests in the Mediterranean area.

The coursers, as you can gather from their name, are strong runners rather than fliers. Both pratincoles and coursers are partial to
hot, dry plains or mud flats. Their nesting habits are much like those
of other shore birds.

## PHALAROPES—THEY WEATHER THE WINTRY GALES

The three species of phalaropes, or sea snipes, are extraordinary birds,
not least in their feeding habits. They have a weird habit of spinning
rapidly round and round in the water when eating. This probably attracts tiny water-dwelling creatures to the surface where the birds
can snap them up with their bills. One observer counted some 250
consecutive turns by a phalarope—which the bird negotiated without
losing its balance!

Phalaropes differ from most birds in their courting and nesting
habits. The male is duller-colored than the female; she is the dominant partner when it comes to courting, while he assumes a coy attitude. Later, the male incubates the eggs and cares for the young by
himself. When they have donned their breeding plumage, phalaropes
—especially the females—have a bright feather pattern of chestnut,
black, and white. This pattern is different for each of the species, but
with the coming of winter they all molt into a dull plumage, leaden
gray above and white below. They are small birds, eight to ten inches
long.

What is perhaps most remarkable of all about the phalaropes is
that, despite their kinship to the shore birds, they are able to live at
sea in the wintertime. Two species, the Northern Phalarope, *Lobipes
lobatus,* and the Red Phalarope, *Phalaropus fulicarius,* nest in the
grim Arctic regions of both hemispheres. The remaining species of the
family Phalaropididae, Wilson's Phalarope, *Steganopus tricolor,* nests
in marshes in the interior of North America. They are well adapted
for life at sea with their weblike toe lobes, flattened legs, and dense,
gull-like plumage. At times they visit American shores during a storm;
as a rule, however, they remain at sea except during nesting time. Our
knowledge of their wintering "grounds" is on the sketchy side, but we
do know that these areas cover vast stretches of southern ocean.

Flocks numbering in the tens of thousands remain at sea for months at a time, feeding on tiny creatures in the sea and weathering the gales with a skill and fortitude that comes naturally to them.

## CRAB PLOVERS

The peculiar Crab Plover, *Dromas ardeola,* differs from other shore birds most sharply in its nesting habits. Instead of the orthodox three or four eggs, it lays a single white egg at the end of a burrow dug by the birds. The young crab plover is reported to remain in this burrow for some time, whereas the young of most shore birds are able to follow their parents around a short time after hatching.

The crab plover, which is placed in the family Dromadidae, lives in sandy areas on the coasts and islands of the Indian Ocean. A long-legged, black-and-white shore bird with a heavy black bill, it feeds on crabs and other small creatures of the shore line.

## THICK-KNEES—SHORE BIRDS WITH A DIFFERENCE

Some birds have misleading names, and you may therefore wonder about the basis for the thick-knee's name. In this case, however, the name is quite accurate, for these birds, also known as stone plovers or stone curlews, are remarkable for their prominent, bulging "knees." Ranging in length from one to two feet, the nine species of the family are modestly colored in gray and brown. They all have three toes, long legs, large eyes, and oval nostrils—other shore birds have slit-like ones. Though they dwell chiefly in the warmer portions of the world, one species nests in England.

Thick-knees—they make up the family Burhinidae—are fond of stony areas bordering rivers and lakes, though we find some kinds on sandy deserts or grassy plains containing a scanty covering of bushes. They take their ease in the shade of bushes by day, going abroad at night to feed. When threatened by a daytime intruder, they sometimes try to hide by stretching out on the ground. They travel or forage alone or in pairs, run swiftly, and fly strongly. Their nest is a depression in the ground in which they lay two or three gray, sparsely spotted eggs. They feed on snails, worms, and insects.

The Noisy Thick-knee, *Burhinus bistratus,* ranges from southern Mexico to northwest Brazil. We have taken this huge "shore bird" of the night on the *llanos* (plains) of Venezuela and Colombia, coming upon it while we were hunting with a jacklight to gather birds for scientific purposes. This thick-knee is most remarkable for its great yellow eyes, large heavy bill, and green legs.

The Great Thick-knee, *Esacus recurvirostris,* of southern Asia stands a foot and one-half high and has a total length of nearly two feet. As we can tell from its scientific name, the heavy, sharply pointed bill is curved upwards.

## SEED SNIPE—THEY FLOCK TOGETHER

These peculiar grouselike birds of South America and the Falkland Islands almost invariably travel in flocks. Such groups sometimes number fifty or more and it is not unusual for them to permit a horseman to ride through their midst without taking flight. When unmolested, the birds creep slowly about, calling to one another with deep pigeon-like whistles. They are crafty when it comes to concealing themselves, and it is very hard to flush them. If, at length, they are flushed, seed snipe rocket upward like snipe, twisting and uttering a sharp grating cry. In the air the flock maintains tight formation and travels with great speed.

We find the strongly migratory seed snipe at sea level in Patagonia, and again up to fourteen thousand feet in the Bolivian Andes. The Patagonian species winters on the pampas of northern Argentina.

Seed snipe range in length from six to twelve inches; the smallest types remind us of quails. The four known species all have comparatively stout bodies, short, weak legs, long and sharply pointed wings, and plumage with a fowl-like texture. Though they make up a very distinct family (the Thinocoridae), seed snipe are cousins of the shore birds.

As their name indicates, seed snipe feed almost exclusively on vegetable matter—mainly seeds. These birds nest in a grass-lined depression in the ground. Here the female deposits three to four pale-gray or pinkish-gray pear-shaped eggs, thickly spotted with brown. Observers have reported that she covers the eggs with grass when she is not incubating them.

## OYSTER CATCHERS

Some bird names, such as the tropic bird and bird of paradise, have romantic connotations. Other names are plain and sternly functional, telling you at once how the bird gets its living. Such a one is the oyster catcher, which does just that: It catches oysters. When feeding, it wades in shallow water and quickly jabs its strong, sharp-edged bill into the opened shell of an oyster or clam, cutting the flesh so that the victim is unable to clamp shut on the bird's bill.

Making up the family Haematopodidae, the six species of oyster catchers—or mussel pickers, as they are called in England—dwell along seacoasts over much of the world. In the Eastern Hemisphere they also wander up large rivers. Sizable and conspicuous shore birds, these oyster catchers usually have black and white plumage with a red bill and legs. Often they travel in flocks.

**A BIRD THAT LIVES ON OYSTERS AND CLAMS**
The oyster catcher, a wading bird of the seacoast, lives on oysters and clams, jabbing its strong, sharp bill into the opened shell of these creatures and paralyzing them. A wary bird, the oyster catcher, it is said, will sometimes carry its eggs away, one at a time, at the approach of an intruder.

The female lays several spotted eggs in a depression in the beach. If a human observer comes too close for comfort, an incubating bird is said to sometimes carry its eggs, one at a time, between its legs to a new location. Normally wary, oyster catchers drop their caution at the approach of an intruder to their nest; they fly about and scream noisily.

The Common Oyster Catcher, *Haematopus ostralegus*, appears on coasts in many parts of the world. On the East coast of North America it nests from Virginia south; in the West the Black Oyster Catcher, a variety of the same species, ranges as far as Alaska.

## SHEATHBILLS—THEY HAVE TO BE RESOURCEFUL

Living in the bleak antarctic wastes, where the sea is the ultimate source of all food, the sheathbills are the only birds in that desolate region without webbed feet. They are bold and aggressive—they have to be. Traveling widely, they visit colonies of penguins and other seafowl, where they are quick to eat any neglected eggs or almost anything else that is edible. Man they hold in so little respect that they may sometimes be picked up by hand.

There are two species of these stocky white birds, not unlike a pigeon in size and appearance. The horny sheath that covers much of the bill gives the birds their name. Though they have no close relatives, we may think of the sheathbill family (Chionidae) as shore birds of rather an unusual kind. The oyster catchers are perhaps their nearest kin.

## GULLS AND TERNS—FROM SALT OCEAN TO SALT LAKE

We think of the gulls and terns as seacoast birds; yet the terns include the world's champion long-distance migrator, while one species of gull has been honored by a monument for valuable services rendered as far inland as Salt Lake City!

However, the gulls and terns do have many physical similarities, and they share many traits in common. For example, they are both elegant and powerful fliers, they have a marked fondness for fish, and many of them nest in large colonies.

## GULLS—VALUABLE SCAVENGERS OF PORT AND HARBOR

Gulls are among the most graceful of all flying birds, and their alternations of wheeling and dipping are a delight to the eye. They spend quite a bit of time resting on the water; thoroughly at home in that element, they swim well, aided by their webbed feet. The slightly curved bill is strong, suitably so for a roving, alert bird that is always on the lookout for a morsel of food.

Gulls are large or medium-sized birds, usually white, though the back and upper surfaces of the wings—usually called the "mantle"

—are often washed with gray or black. In many gulls we observe that the head is black during the nesting season, and often we see black marks on the flight feathers. Gulls and terns are placed in the family Laridae.

**The Herring Gull or Common Sea Gull,** *Larus argentatus,* is the most familiar of all the gulls. An avid scavenger of all kinds of garbage and refuse, it will eat almost anything in the way of food. Its resourcefulness is proverbial; it will probe for mussels with its bill, snatch them up, soar some fifty feet in the air, drop them to the ground to smash the shells, and extract the contents. It has been known to snatch fish stuck in a pelican's bill.

We always find gulls in quantity along coasts, in harbors, near fishing vessels. It has been calculated that there are seventy-five thousand gulls in New York Harbor, where they render a valuable service in mitigating pollution by consuming large amounts of refuse. Despite their scavenging habits, they are exceptionally clean birds.

Gulls survive the fiercest storms at sea, and they rest by sleeping on the waves. They get along well on land, too, and flourish in the severest extremes of climate.

Large nesting colonies are the rule for herring gulls. They lay their three heavily marked eggs in a crude nest of seaweed. They make solicitous parents but may be very harsh toward the young of other gulls. While they are generally sociable creatures, they can be very quarrelsome at times. The baby gulls announce they are hungry by tapping a red spot on the grownups' bills.

Years ago thousands of gulls used to be killed for their feathers, but now the birds are protected by law. Partly because of this protection, partly because of the growth of great seaports surrounded by garbage dumps, the gulls have multiplied enormously. In Maine and Canada the authorities control the herring gull colonies by gathering the eggs or spraying them with a strong chemical. On Bonaventure Island in the Gulf of St. Lawrence, where we found this gull nesting in scattered colonies on the rocky shores, it was very destructive to the eggs and young of the local members of the auk family. In other places it preys on eider ducks, terns, or other more desirable species—so we see there is a real need for rigorous control.

The herring gull is one of the largest birds of the gull clan. Up to twenty-six inches long, it has a wingspread of almost five feet. Its flying speed is about thirty-five miles an hour.

**The Franklin Gull,** *Larus pipixcan,* is one of the gulls that nest inland, though it is true that gulls are commonest on seacoasts. It feeds chiefly on insects which it catches in flight or on the ground. To this trait it owes its famous Salt Lake City monument—a tall marble shaft topped by a ball on which two gulls have just landed. About a hundred years ago a plague of crickets threatened to destroy the crops of the pioneer Mormons who had recently arrived in the West. The menaced crops were saved by flocks of Franklin and California gulls which wiped out the pestiferous insects by what must have seemed like a miracle to the farmers.

Although several kinds of gulls are migratory, the Franklin gull is the only northern species to penetrate into the Southern Hemisphere. "Prairie pigeon" is another name given to this bird in the interior of the United States. It breeds in large colonies on marshes, and lays two or three eggs.

**The Great Black-backed Gull,** *Larus marinus,* is the largest of all the gulls. Reaching a total length of thirty inches, it has a wingspread to sixty-six inches. Timid in man's presence, it is a bold robber of other

**THE LARGEST GULL**
The good-looking black-backed gull, some thirty inches long with a wingspread of sixty-six inches, is the largest of all the gulls. This gull is as resourceful as its cousins when it comes to obtaining food, and boldly steals from other birds.

birds' food and eggs. You can readily distinguish its deep-pitched cries from the raucous screaming of the herring gull or the noisy gabble of the Laughing Gull or other lesser species. In recent years this handsome bird has nested on the eastern coast of Long Island in New York but its stronghold is much further north.

At the other extreme in size is the Little Gull, *Larus minutus,* a bird of European and Asiatic waters. Of late years it has appeared in small numbers every winter in eastern North America.

Most gulls, as we have seen, are hardy birds. A case in point is that of the Rosy Gull, *Rhodostethia rosa,* which nests in the Arctic regions and apparently winters along open leads of water in the Arctic Ocean. Like many gulls and terns, it has a beautiful rosy bloom on the breast.

The Bonaparte Gull, *Larus philadelphia,* another species that breeds in the north, builds its nest in the tops of spruce trees instead of on the ground as other gulls do. Its young remain in the nest, unlike the young of other gulls, which scramble about near their nest. (Baby gulls, however, are by no means the equals of most young shore birds when it comes to running.) The Bonaparte gull is about fourteen inches long, with a wingspread up to thirty-two inches. When it travels further south it destroys a great many insects, sometimes on the wing, in the inland regions where it lives a good deal.

## TERNS—THEY INCLUDE THE CHAMPION MIGRATOR

**The Arctic Tern,** *Sterna paradisaea,* is famous for its annual round-trip migratory flight of some twenty-two thousand miles—the longest migration of any known creature. The individuals undertaking this amazing journey first enjoy nearly four months of continuous daylight on their breeding grounds during the Arctic summer, followed by four months of almost continuous daylight on their Antarctic wintering grounds. These birds live to within eight degrees of the North Pole during their Arctic sojourn. However, some birds of this species nest as far south as Massachusetts—nor do they all reach the Antarctic during their migrations. In appearance the Arctic tern is typical of this tribe of water-loving birds. White below and gray above, it has a black cap, and scarlet legs and bill.

Terns are so graceful in flight that we sometimes call them "sea swallows." There are forty-five species of these small to medium-sized gull-like birds. They have a long, straight, slender bill, long, tapering wings, and a forked tail.

As we have seen, some terns do not indulge in extended migratory flights; they favor coastal regions in warm latitudes. They usually nest in colonies, laying one to three white eggs mottled with dark brown, in slight hollows scraped in the sand. A few species, such as the White-capped Noddy, *Anous minutus,* build nests of seaweed on bushes. (According to some naturalists, this bird gets its curious name from its exceptional tameness and "stupidity." Others believe the name comes from a habit this tern has of nodding on meeting a fellow tern.) The Fairy or Love Tern, *Gygis alba,* precariously balances its single spotted egg on the gnarled bark of a horizontal limb in a tree. The Inca Tern, *Larosterna inca,* which dwells on the Peruvian coast, places its egg in a rock niche high above the water.

Terns feed on small fish obtained by diving. A few take insects on the wing. Unlike gulls, terns are not scavengers. Female and male look alike in size and coloration. Several kinds of terns are black or brown, but most of them are white. They usually sport a black or gray cap.

At the close of the last century many tern colonies were wiped out by feather collectors and eggers. Aided by adequate protection, these graceful birds have increased greatly.

### SKIMMERS—THEY CLEAVE THE WATER

Long-winged relatives of the terns, skimmers differ from all other birds in having a vertically flattened, knifelike bill. It was this feature that gave them the nickname of "scissorbills." The lower half of this bill is much longer than the upper. Skimmers also differ from other birds in their eye structure; they have vertical, slitlike pupils.

Skimmers fly low over the water with the bladelike bill plowing or cleaving the surface. In this way they are able to seize small marine organisms and fish which come into contact with the moving, open bill.

**The American Black Skimmer,** *Rhynchops nigra,* is predominantly black; the forehead, and the sides of the face and under parts are white. The tip of the bill is black, the legs red. The female skimmer lays three or four handsome eggs, buff with irregular black blotches, in little hollows which the bird has scraped in the sand by a rotating action of her breast. These eggs are tasty, and fishermen used to frequently make off with them. The generally inoffensive skimmers are always bold and noisy in the nesting area, uttering cries not unlike those of a pack of yelping terriers.

**THE "SCISSORBILL" BIRD**

The skimmer's bill does not have its like in any other bird. Vertically flattened like a knife, this bill has earned the skimmer the nickname of "scissorbill." When you see the skimmer flying low over the surface, you can appreciate the effectiveness of this bill as it cleaves the water and seizes small fish and marine organisms.

The American skimmer frequents the east coast of the United States, and we find it as far south as Argentina. For a long time this bird shunned the coasts of Massachusetts and Long Island, New York; it has since resumed nesting in colonies in those areas. The family Rhynchopidae includes the American skimmer and two other species of skimmers—one in Africa, one in India—that live along the banks of large rivers.

## JAÇANAS OR LOTUS BIRDS—"LILY-TROTTERS"

Swamps, lagoons, and sluggish streams choked with floating vegetation are the home of the seven species of jaçanas, or lotus birds. They are remarkable birds in a number of ways—above all, in the fantastic length of their toes and claws. Usually very flexible and often curved up rather than down, this specialized footwear enables the jaçana to run over the filmiest of plant rafts without sinking. This trait inspired someone with a sense of humor to dub the jaçana a "lily-trotter." The hind toenail of the Lotus Bird or Combcrested Jaçana, *Irediparra gallinacea,* of Australia, is three and one-quarter inches long!

Jaçanas dwell in the warmer portions of the world. Slender birds with a long, tightly feathered neck and body, they have gangly legs and well-developed wing spurs. The body is no larger than a robin's. These birds are shy, but they fly vigorously. Upon alighting, they hold the wings elevated for a moment, as do many shore birds. In the air they let their long legs and toes trail nearly horizontally behind them. Their fare is made up of water insects, mollusks, and plants. These birds are grouped in the family Jacanidae.

**LILY-TROTTER AND LOTUS BIRD**
These are two of the names given the jaçana, a bird which spends much of its life on floating vegetation. Jaçanas have long toes and claws to enable them to run across the most delicate water plants without sinking. One species has a hind toenail more than three inches long. The pheasant-tailed jaçana, pictured above, has a tail a foot long.

Though similar in color, the female jaçana is about twice as large as her mate—so you will not be surprised to learn that by human standards the male is a henpecked creature, burdened with most of the domestic chores. The nest is generally a flat—sometimes a cup-shaped—structure, made of slender-leafed water plants and in some cases of considerable size. It is often placed in short matted grass close over water, and on occasion left partially afloat. The two to four glossy eggs are buffy, cinnamon, or even green with scroll-like black markings.

The American Jaçana, *Jacana spinosa,* lives in tropical America as far north as southern Texas. A deep reddish-maroon bird, it has pale apple-green wings, while its head and neck are greenish black. The orange wattle on the forehead adds still another color to the ensemble. The species name *spinosa* refers to the sharp, horny wing spurs which the bird probably uses for fighting.

The Pheasant-tailed Jaçana, *Hydrophasianus* ("water pheasant") of tropical Asia, is the largest as well as the most peculiar of these peculiar birds. Its tail is more than a foot long. The dark areas of its gaudy plumage are purplish maroon; the light areas are white, except on the hind neck, which is glossy gold.

## AUKS, MURRES, PUFFINS, AND THEIR RELATIVES

These birds dwell on the desolate seas and islands of the Northern Hemisphere, mostly within the Subarctic or Arctic Zones. They get their food in a remarkable way—they seize fish and crustaceans by diving from the surface and "flying" under the water. No less than nineteen of the twenty-two species of this family, the Alcidae, are present at some time of the year along American coasts. In the East none nest south of Maine, but in the West two species nest on islands in the Gulf of California. In winter some auks wander farther south.

### AUKS—BULLET-LIKE FLIERS

In habits and appearance auks are the northern equivalent of the penguins of the Antarctic. However, the auks are smaller birds and all surviving species are able to fly. Thus they are less highly specialized for ocean life. Nevertheless, auks spend much of the year at sea, gathered in loose flocks. They fly in bullet-like fashion with rapid wing beats, usually staying together in flocks or strings and frequently bar-reling down to the water with great clumsy splashes like a skipped stone as they dash after fish. In the spring, when they establish large nesting colonies on oceanic islands, and later in the year on the win-tering grounds, it is customary for several species to consort together.

Although we find several interesting auks in the Atlantic, their real stronghold is the North Pacific. There, on the bleak coasts of the Aleutian Islands, a great variety of species turn up in countless throngs. Many of them are grotesquely ornamented with whisker-like facial plumes or growths on the head. The Ancient Murrelet, the Rhi-noceros Auklet, and the Horned Puffin—creatures as quaint as their names—will be among those greeting the naturalist who visits this region.

## MURRES AND THEIR GROWLING MOANS

Breeding murres and auks are strangely tame and as one wanders among them, as we did on Funk Island off the north coast of New-foundland in 1936, they keep up a constant growling moan. With their black upper parts and heads and gleaming white breasts, they remind us of a convention of disgruntled waiters.

The Common and Brunnich's Murres, *Uria aalge* and *Uria lomvia,* lay a single, relatively huge, pear-shaped egg, blotched variably with black and brown. They build no nest; the egg remains on the ground and, because it is cone-shaped, rolls no farther than the radius of a small circle. The downy young murres have sooty and grayish breasts. Their parents feed them by regurgitation.

## PUFFINS—COMICAL BUT ADROIT

**The Atlantic Puffin,** *Fratercula arctica,* is a comical-looking bird with its rather large black head with a gray collar, its disproportionately large, stubby blue and crimson bill, its white cheeks and under parts, and its red legs that afford it nothing better than a clumsy waddling gait. The harsh croak is what might be expected from this grotesque figure. For all its whimsical appearance, the puffin is quite business-like in its fishing technique. Whenever we saw a puffin with its usual catch of five to ten smelt, each hanging limply by its gills from the bird's bill, we marveled at the puffin's ability to seize additional fish without dropping those previously captured. The bill, by the way, has an outer shell that the bird sheds and then grows anew each year.

Puffins dig nesting burrows in the earth and line them with a crude nest of feathers and grass. The single whitish egg is incubated for nearly five weeks, both parents taking part.

**THE GROTESQUE PUFFIN**
Few birds can match the clownish appearance of the Atlantic puffin. It has a big black head, an oversized blue and crimson bill, white under parts, and red legs. The comical effect is enhanced by its clumsy waddle and harsh croak. The puffin replaces the outer shell of its bill each year.

## THE GREAT AUK—MADE EXTINCT BY WHOLESALE SLAUGHTER

Much has been written about the North Atlantic Penguin, Garefowl or Great Auk, *Pinguinus impennis*, the largest and only flightless member of the family Alcidae. The very last great auk was killed more than a century ago (1844). Yet only a few years before that they abounded in the waters of the North Atlantic, breeding by the thousands on the islets off the coast of Newfoundland, Greenland, Iceland, and the Orkneys. Today this remarkable bird, aside from the accounts of early travelers, is known to us only from a few stuffed birds, eggs, and skeletons. Total extinction was visited upon the great auk with such amazing rapidity largely because of its almost suicidal instinct to return to its ancestral breeding grounds. Here the sealers slaughtered it both for its oil and its plumage.

On Funk Island, one of the last homes of the great auk, we unearthed some seven thousand bones in less than five hours during our brief visit in 1936. All but a handful were those of the great auk, which gives you some idea of the magnitude of the slaughter that took place three generations ago. Here it was that we came upon stone corrals or pens, with walls averaging about two and one-half feet high, into which the great flightless birds were herded like sheep to be slaughtered and defeathered in huge caldrons heated by the burning bodies of their fatty brethren. Jacques Cartier, who first discovered this colony in 1535, recorded in his log the restocking of the ship's larder with great auks.

## DOVEKIES—SMALLEST OF THE FAMILY

At the other extreme in size from the great auk is the Dovekie, *Plautus alle,* about nine inches long. The Eskimos catch great numbers of dovekies in nets on the nesting cliffs. The birds are then stuffed into sealskin bags and cached away until winter.

The dovekie is black above, white below, and has a white streak above the eye. Rarely do dovekies get as far south as the United States except during influx years when, as in November, 1932, a great wave of them surged down the coast, and even spread some distance inland. Most of these birds probably perished.

# Pigeons, Doves, Dodos, and Sand Grouse

THIS ORDER, which includes one of the best known of all birds, also has the melancholy distinction of containing two famous birds that were exterminated by man. One of them was so far away from our conception of a bird that it has taken on the proportions of a mythical creature; the other was indeed a typical bird, the most abundant in North America according to some; the most abundant in the world, according to others. The pigeons, doves, and their relatives make up the order Columbiformes.

## PIGEONS AND DOVES

This is a large family—some 290 species, including the popular Domestic Pigeon or Rock Dove, *Columba livia*. If you are familiar with this famous citizen of the bird world, you would have little difficulty recognizing almost any pigeon or dove as belonging to this family, known as the Columbidae: for they all have the same soft, sleek, rather small and rounded head, plump, full-breasted body, and short, soft-skinned legs and toes. The bill is slender and partly covered with a fine growth ("cere"). Dense, smooth feathers are loosely attached, especially on the back. They loosen a cloud of feathers when pursued by a falcon thereby confusing the enemy and sometimes escaping.

### THE DIFFERENCE BETWEEN DOVES AND PIGEONS

What is the difference between "doves" and "pigeons"? None, really, though we use the former term more often for the smaller, gentler members of the family—the symbolic "dove of peace." Weakly represented in the Northern Hemisphere, this group is much more numerous in the tropics of America and Africa. In Australia, New Guinea, and on the Pacific islands these birds are found in greater variety and profusion of species than elsewhere in the world.

1035

## WAYS OF THE PIGEONS

The ardent cooing and strutting of the male pigeon of our parks are typical of the whole family. Equally characteristic are the notes of these birds, with their almost invariably soft cooing or hooting quality, the melancholy effect often enhanced by monotonous repetition. Mated pigeons are deeply attached to each other, and if one of a pair dies it will take some time before the other takes a new mate.

All pigeons lay unspotted white or buffy eggs. All the better-known kinds lay two eggs in a set, but a few tropical species lay only one. The nest is a flimsy, untidy structure. Both parents incubate, the male usually by day and his mate by night. After the young hatch, they are fed on "pigeon's milk"—a unique substance secreted by the lining of the parent's crop and then pumped into the mouths of the young. This feeding method is comparable to the mammals' and is unlike any found in other birds. The pigeon's ability to drink without lifting its head to swallow is a trait found in few other groups.

Most pigeons are strong, swift fliers. This, together with their palatable flesh, makes them favorite game birds in many parts of the world. Pigeons reproduce too slowly to be shot at random, but game hunting threatens to exterminate many species. In desert regions they are often shot as they make their flights to water holes.

The "Carrier" or "Homing" Pigeon (one of the numerous varieties of the domestic species) is famous for its homing feats. Actually, it has less homing ability than many wild birds! With training, however, it quickly becomes proficient. Speeds of about sixty miles an hour are common, and the maximum homing distance is in the neighborhood of twelve hundred miles.

## AMERICAN PIGEONS AND DOVES

**The Passenger Pigeon,** *Ectopistes migratorius,* became extinct in 1914 when the last known bird of this species died in the Zoological Gardens at Cincinnati. Back in 1605 the French explorer Samuel de Champlain observed passenger pigeons in "infinite numbers" in Maine. In the days of the young Republic, these birds perched on trees in such dense groups that they broke the boughs by sheer weight. Migratory flocks, miles long, darkened the sun and took hours to pass a given point. Alexander Wilson, the "Father of American ornithology," estimated that one such throng observed by him near Frankfort, Kentucky, about the year 1808, contained over two billion passenger pigeons. And yet we know that by the turn of the century these birds had become very scarce. What had happened in the intervening years?

Man was the culprit. First he mass-slaughtered the passenger pigeons for food for himself, then for pigs, even bringing the swine to the roosting places to devour the victims. It was fantastically easy to shoot the birds, but it was cheaper and quicker to blind them with torches and club them to death, or to suffocate them by burning sulphur under their roosts. Thus these once abundant birds were wiped out.

**The Mourning Dove,** *Zenaidura macroura,* is the only common species over most of the northern United States and Canada now that the passenger pigeon is gone. Also known as the Turtle Dove, the mourning dove does not nest in dense colonies as did the passenger pigeons, and so has survived in goodly numbers. Mourning doves, when mated, are among the most affectionate honeymooners in the bird kingdom, and their absorption in each other is proverbial. Apparently they give little attention to such practical matters as nest-building, for the structure is usually a flimsy affair, set up without an eye to the best shelter and protection. The two white eggs are consequently at the mercy of crows, snakes, cats, and other enemies. Perhaps as nature's way of making up for these hazards, the doves produce two or more broods during the mating season.

Mourning doves feed mostly on seeds, which does not endear them to the prosaic farmer. They have a familiar call of "coo-wee-oo, coo-o-o, coo-o-o, coo-o-o," which may strike you as gentle or mournful, depending on your mood. These birds spend the winter in Mexico and the southern states.

The appearance of the mourning dove is quite similar to its vanished cousin's, but the passenger pigeon was somewhat larger and had a strong reddish tint on its breast. A slender bird, the mourning dove is brownish, tinted with lavender. The tail is pointed and you can see the large white spots near its tip when the bird takes off or alights. Whenever the mourning dove springs into the air its wings beat together noisily—a characteristic of many doves.

In the southern United States the little Ground Dove, *Columbigallina passerina,* often flutters up under foot. You can recognize it easily by its small size—a seven-inch length is the maximum—and its chestnut wing patches. A slightly larger species, the Inca Dove, *Scardafella inca,* is common in the gardens of Tucson, Arizona, and other southwestern cities. Its repetitious two-syllabled call, sounding like "wa-hoo," can be heard even during the noontime hush of a summer's day, when the heat has lulled every other bird into silence.

## EXOTIC PIGEONS OF THE TROPICS

The tropics abound in many colorful or unusual pigeons. The Fruit Doves of the Polynesian islands (genus *Ptilinopus*) are among the loveliest of all birds. The top of the head is often violet, and the rest of the color pattern consists of softly blended pastel shades of green, yellow, and lavender. As we can gather from the common name of

**A PIGEON OF THE TROPICS**

The crowned pigeon, a bird of New Guinea, is the largest member of the pigeon family and also one of the handsomest. In common with other pigeons, it feeds its young on "pigeon milk"—a fluid secreted in the lining of the parent's crop and then pumped into the babies' mouths. This technique is practiced by no other bird. Because of its curiosity and fearlessness, the crowned pigeon is doomed wherever man settles.

these birds, they live chiefly on wild fruits. This is also true of most members of the family, though many species include seeds and nuts, as well as fruit, in their fare.

Pigeons are noted for their soft, smooth plumage, but the Nicobar Pigeon, *Caloenas nicobarica,* is an exception; it has long, loose, pointed feathers that give it a shaggy appearance. The plumage is blackish, glossed with purple and bronzy reflections, and the tail is white.

The largest members of the family Columbidae are the Crowned Pigeons, *Goura,* of New Guinea, which are the size of a large chicken. They are handsome birds with maroon body plumage, gray wings, and a pearly crest of lacy head plumes running the length of the crown.

## DODOS AND SOLITAIRES

Twice as large as a goose, flightless, with thick stubby legs and long "pants," a poodle-like tail complete with curls, tight pigeon-like body plumage, a tremendous skull equipped with a stout, heavily plated and deeply hooked bill, a naked face and dog-sized mouth, the Dodo, *Didus ineptus,* was perhaps the most un-birdlike bird that ever lived.

Extinct for centuries, the dodo yet contrives to hold its place as one of the best known of birds—possibly because so many of us are introduced to it at an early age by reading *Alice in Wonderland.* The bird was first discovered by the Portuguese in 1507 and last seen alive in 1681. Thereafter it lapsed into the realm of fantasy. Most people took a skeptical view of the early sketches and accounts which depicted so preposterous a creature—this despite the fact that a number of live dodos were brought to Europe early in the seventeenth century.

What traces of the dodo remain? Specimens of the head and feet are preserved at Oxford, and a number of skeletal parts are scattered around the world in collections. In 1907 the American Museum of Natural History acquired the bones of a dodo in a swap for the skeleton of a Right Whale.

The true dodo lived on the island of Mauritius in the Indian Ocean, about five hundred miles east of Madagascar. Another species, *Didus borbonicus,* was found about a hundred miles away from Mauritius on the island of Réunion, while the Solitaire, *Pezophaps solitarius,* a smaller, less peculiar dodo, made its home on nearby Rodriguez Island.

All these birds, which made up the family Raphidae, are extinct but, luckily, a few hints of their habits were recorded before their early disappearance. From these accounts we gather that the dodos—now acknowledged to have been monstrous, flightless pigeons—lived in deep forest, walked with a ludicrous waddle, and laid one large egg which both parents incubated. They swallowed gizzard stones as large as chicken eggs and sported a rounded knuckle or knob of bone on the bend of the wing. This may have been a handy weapon for squabbling among themselves, but it was of no avail against the pigs introduced by early settlers on these islands. The pigs evidently feasted on the eggs and young birds, and the phrase "dead as a dodo" soon became a tragic reality.

## SAND GROUSE

At intervals two or three Asiatic kinds of sand grouse embark on no-madic wanderings like the lemmings', reaching western Europe and even the British Isles. When the wanderlust subsides, the migrants make no attempt to return. Instead, they try to nest in whatever re-

**PALLAS'S SAND GROUSE—BIRD OF THE DESERT**
Pallas's sand grouse lives on the high, cold steppes of central Asia, where its dense plumage protects it from the low temperatures. Its feathered feet may help support it on the desert sands. Sand grouse of Asia occasionally wander to western Europe and, instead of returning home, try to establish themselves in their new surroundings.

gion they find themselves. In a few years, tragically, all these birds disappear. Yet even in their homeland their lives are beset with danger. Like desert pigeons, sand grouse fly long distances to and from water holes. In India the maharajahs, familiar with this trait, place hunting blinds near water holes and shoot enormous numbers of sand grouse in winter, when the breeding birds of central Asia are wintering there.

The sixteen species of sand grouse make up a small but interesting family, the Pteroclidae. In appearance they fall between the quails and the pigeons. Though sand grouse are probably related to the pigeons, their spotted eggs and downy chicks look quite unlike pigeons'. Protectively colored, they present a blending pattern of brown, buff, gray, white, and black to match the desert sands. The adult birds have a slender, trim appearance, enhanced by a pointed tail. They fly rapidly.

# Parrots—Long-lived and Loquacious

YOU MAY RECALL that Long John Silver had a parrot named Captain Flint. The bird often called out "Pieces of eight!" Sometimes it would "swear straight on, passing belief for wickedness." According to Long John, Captain Flint was "maybe" two hundred years old. The parrot had traveled widely—"Madagascar, and at Malabar, and Surinam, and Providence, and Portobello."

If you stop to think about it, you will realize that the parrot is a stock figure in sea stories of bygone times. Parrots are not native to Europe or nontropical Asia; most of the 315 species dwell in the warmer and less accessible parts of the world. The possession of this exotic bird was the sailor's documentary proof, so to speak, of the romantic isles he had visited. And then, the bird was fascinating in its own right—for its ability to "talk," its longevity, the arrangement of its claws which permits it to "handle" food. For lonely sailors, the saucy, sociable, cynical parrot is ideal company.

Though we associate parrots with warm climates, it is interesting to observe that fossil discoveries indicate the former presence of parrots in Europe and nontropical Asia. There are all sorts of parrots. They range in size from about the dimensions of a small sparrow to the large macaws, some three feet long. All of them are members of the order Psittaciformes and remarkably similar in basic form. Predominantly green, their dress is varied by the addition of red, yellow, blue, white, and black. Long plumes of exquisite color and design enhance the colorful effect.

The powerful, sharply hooked bill—the parrot's most characteristic feature—is often deeply notched. The lower half of the bill is short, stocky, and sharply upcurved. It is fastened to the skull by transverse ligaments similar to those of the human jaw. The parrot's neck is short, the head relatively large. In the feet we note a remarkable structure—they are "yoke-toed," with the first and fourth toes extending backward, and they are used like a hand for holding food. This accomplishment is shared by few other birds. As you would expect, parrots walk and climb with sureness and ease, thanks to this arrangement.

These birds fly powerfully, almost always in pairs or flocks, and usually to the accompaniment of raucous, discordant screams. They hiss when defending their nest; at other times they utter shrill whistles. In the wild state they do not imitate other birds or animals. But in captivity, as we know, many species imitate human speech—even laughter or crying, as well as the barking of dogs and the coughing of children. Stories are told of parrots being able to recite the Lord's Prayer and the Apostles' Creed, and it is said that the testimony of parrots has been given partial though not decisive credence in a number of court trials. It seems that the first writer to allude to the parrot's powers of mimicry was Ctesias (about 400 B.C.) in his description of captive African parrots brought to Greece at that early date. In Nero's day the Romans kept parrots in cages of tortoise shell and silver.

The talking ability, longevity (anywhere from fifteen to eighty years), docility, and humor of the parrot have understandably made it one of our best-loved caged birds. Still, because parrots occasionally carry the once deadly psittacosis ("parrot disease"), their importation was barred until recently. Ornithosis is a better name for this rare virus disease, as it may be transmitted by several kinds of birds. Fortunately the disease has yielded to the modern antibiotics, and parakeets are now almost a fad.

Certain species, such as the African Gray Parrot and the green *Amazona* parrots of South America, have become especially famous as "talkers." Bear in mind, however, that individual birds vary greatly—some learn readily, others "ain't talking."

**A PARROT WITH A RACKET-SHAPED TAIL**
This medium-sized grass-green parrot was named for its two curiously shaped central tail feathers, which are rather like those of the motmot. The racket-tailed parrot dwells in flocks in the Philippines, where it frequents the tops of lofty jungle trees.

With the exception of one South American species that builds a bulky nest of grass and twigs in a tree, parrots lay their eggs in cavities which they scoop out themselves or appropriate from other birds. The cavity may be in rotting wood, in termite nests, under roots, in earthen burrows, or in crevices in cliffs. Parrots rarely use nesting material. Their eggs are white, the larger species laying two to three and the smaller ones up to a dozen. When it comes to incubating, the male usually cooperates in the task. The young are quite helpless at birth and are fed by regurgitation. More than one brood may be reared in a season. It often happens that several families of parrots live in a single tree; as we have seen, parrots are sociable birds. Their daily movements to and from a roost are features of the tropical forest, and old-timers will insist that a clock may be set by their noisy, punctual travels. Parrots feed mainly on nuts, seeds, and fruits.

**The Papuan Lory,** *Vini papou,* which we have observed and collected in southern New Guinea, is typical of the brush-tongued lories of the Australian region. Traveling in flocks in the forest crown, it often perches in the extreme tip limbs of great isolated trees. The beautiful central tail plumes are green on their basal halves and light ocher-yellow on the outer third. The bill and legs are orange scarlet, while the body is largely crimson with the wings, central back, and base of the tail bright green; glossy blue patches occur on the hind crown and rump. To complete this riot of color, the hind crown and shanks or "pants" are jet black. These lories use their brushy tongue in feeding on the nectar of flowers.

**The Pygmy Parrot,** *Micropsitta,* is an unbelievable creature, smaller than a Downy Woodpecker and rather similar in shape. It has the stiff spiny tail—useful as a prop—of the woodpecker, and the feet are adapted for climbing on the trunks of trees. The pygmy parrot is a green bird with black crown and ochraceous cheeks.

**The Sulphur-crested Cockatoo,** *Cacatua galerita,* and the **Great Black Cockatoo,** *Probosciger aterrimus,* are probably the noisiest birds of the New Guinea forests and the best examples of the cockatoos of the Australian region. But, vociferous as they are, they are extremely difficult to approach because of their wary and suspicious nature; they are said to post sentinels.

The great black cockatoo is bluish black and has partially naked cheeks. This feature, its tremendous crest, and massive sickle-bill make it quite conspicuous. The bird uses the bill to tear large grubs from rotting wood and to probe kernels of fruit. It is perhaps the largest of all parrots.

**The Red, Blue, and Green Macaw,** *Ara chloroptera,* is typical of the large macaws that dwell in tropical America. This brilliant bird ranges from Panama to Bolivia. Its principal colors are evident from its name, and it has a number of cousins that are every bit as gaudy. With their huge strong bills they can easily crack a Brazil nut and then cleverly extract the meat with the hooked bill and the tongue. Macaws nest in holes in cliffs as well as in hollow trees.

**GAUDY BIRD OF TROPICAL AMERICA**
The macaw of tropical America is one of the most brilliantly colored of all the parrots. So strong is the huge hooked bill that the macaw has no trouble cracking a Brazil nut and getting out the meat by manipulating the pieces with its tongue and bill.

**The African Gray Parrot,** *Psittacus erithacus,* is one of the best known of the almost infinite variety of parrots. Famous as a talking bird, it has been shipped abroad in countless numbers. In captivity these birds have been known to survive as long as eighty years. Their coloring is rather subdued for parrots—ashy gray, with red tail feathers.

**The Carolina Parakeet,** *Conuropis carolinensis,* was wiped out during the present century through excessive hunting by "sportsmen," plume hunters, and farmers. This handsome little parrot, which was yellow and green, with a pointed tail, formerly ranged over much of the southern United States. The late Dr. Frank M. Chapman found a colony of some fifty of these parakeets on the Sebastian River in eastern Florida, and in April, 1904, he saw thirteen on Lake Okeechobee.

So far as we know, the species has not been seen since. Like some other parrots, it was occasionally destructive to fruit, and was often shot for this reason.

## LOVEBIRDS AND THEIR RELATIVES

The lovebirds are small Old World parrots, greatly prized as cage birds for their endearing ways. They are so affectionate that they sit together, often with chests and heads touching. One of the most popular and best known is the Rose-faced Lovebird of Africa, *Agapornis roseicollis.* Though the bird is mostly green, it has a red forehead and tail, while the sides of the head and neck are rose. An astonishing trait of these birds is their habit of pushing grass or other nesting material beneath the feathers of their backs and thus carrying it to the nesting burrow in a tree. Other well-known members of the family are the Australian Bruderigar, *Melopsittacus,* which is greenish striped with black, though blue and white varieties have been developed; and the charming little Bat Parrots of the Philippines, which get their name from their strange habit of hanging head downward while slumbering.

## OTHER REMARKABLE PARROTS

The blunt-tailed parrots, *Amazona,* are perhaps the most famous of all New World parrots. Gifted talkers and many of them nearly as large as a crow, these birds are mainly green with some red or yellow marks. They range from Mexico to Argentina.

Another notable talking species is the Short-tailed Parrot, *Graydidascalus brachyurus,* of northern South America. A great favorite with the Arecuna Indians of the Guiana highlands, this funny little bird waddles about like a tiny old man. Its upper parts are green, the crown and tail black, the flight quills deep blue with narrow greenish edging, the throat and shanks pale yellow, the chest, hind collar, and abdomen buffy white.

The New Zealand Kea, *Nestor notabilis,* selects living quarters that are quite incongruous for a tropical bird. Disdaining the steaming tropics preferred by its cousins, the kea dwells high in the New Zealand Alps, nesting in rocky cliffs in mid-winter. The bird has a powerful hooked bill which it uses to grub out roots. Unfortunately, when goaded by hunger, it also uses this weapon occasionally to rip open the back of a sheep. Aside from this one shortcoming, the kea is a charming bird, inquisitive to the point of fearing neither man nor beast.

**The Owl Parrot,** *Strigops,* another resident of New Zealand, is if any-thing even more interesting than the kea. The owl parrot cannot fly; it is strictly a ground-dweller. It has the disposition of a bright, lively puppy, and it is so appreciative of kind treatment that it rubs and climbs on its benefactor. Its face looks somewhat like an Eng-lish sheep dog's, while its general shape is not unlike a Snowy Owl's —hence the name, owl parrot. The two birds are about equal in size, too, but the owl parrot has green plumage, marked with brown and buff.

Formerly this bird was abundant on both North and South Island of New Zealand; now it is found in only remote mountain forests. Making its home in rocky forests, it lays two or three white eggs in earthen burrows. Both parents share the task of incubating the eggs, which take three weeks to hatch. The owl parrot hides under roots and in cavities by day, becoming active in late evening and night. It feeds on grass, weeds, fallen fruit, and seeds. Roaming dogs are now the owl parrot's worst enemy.

# Cuckoos and Turacos

THERE ARE cuckoos and cuckoos. Few birds are as disliked as these for their reputed habit of laying their eggs in other birds' nests. What many of us fail to realize, however, is that only one of the New World species is guilty of shunting off the duties of parent-hood on its fellow birds; equally little known is the fact that many cuckoos render a valuable service to man by eating vast quantities of injurious insects.

It is the Old World cuckoos that have given this bird a bad name, for many of them are in truth guilty of parasitism. No matter how we feel about this behavior, we cannot help being fascinated by the migrations of the Bronzed Cuckoo, *Chalcites lucidus,* of the Southwest Pacific. The parasitic habits of these birds give rise to one of the most remarkable—and most baffling—of all bird migrations. At their summering grounds in New Zealand, these birds lay their eggs in the nest of flycatchers. The foster parents—they are not migrators —raise the intruders. When fledged, the orphaned young cuckoos fly without hesitation over twelve hundred miles of water to Australia, thence northward another 950 miles to the Solomon and Bismarck Islands, there miraculously joining their parents, who have preceded them there!

## CUCKOOS—NOT ALL ARE PARASITES

As we have seen, many Old World cuckoos are parasitic: they lay their eggs in the nests of other birds, usually one to a nest. Cuckoo eggs require a shorter period of incubation. Once hatched, the young cuckoos grow more rapidly than their nest-mates, are usually larger than they, and have an instinctive urge to hoist them out of the nest. You can forecast the likely result: the destruction of the young birds that rightfully belong in the nest.

Some naturalists once believed that the females of parasitic cuckoos first lay the egg and then place it with their bill in the nest of the foster parent. This theory has never been confirmed. What happens is that these female cuckoos carefully hunt for the nests of small birds and then stealthily lay one of their own eggs in it at an opportune moment. After laying the egg, the hen cuckoo takes no further interest in the fate of her egg or her offspring.

However, as far as the New World cuckoos are concerned, with one exception they all build nests and rear their own young.

There are some 130 species in the cuckoo family, the Cuculidae. As regards size, they range all the way from the size of a sparrow to that of a pheasant. We find them around the globe, but they are most numerous and diverse in the African and Indo-Malayan tropics. The brighter birds in the family are brilliantly colored; a few have gaudy accessory plumes. The great majority of cuckoos, however, are brownish with the under parts barred, the tail rounded with white tips, and the bill strong and curved.

When winter comes, the cuckoos, living as they do largely on insects, must migrate to the tropics if they live in the Northern Hemisphere. For example, both the Black-billed and Yellow-billed Cuckoos of the United States migrate to South America every year. Even on its home grounds, the cuckoo is a shy, furtive bird. You are more likely to hear its famous characteristic cry than you are to see it in the flesh.

### TRUE CUCKOOS—SOME OF THEM RESEMBLE HAWKS

True cuckoos make their homes in the forests of the Old World. Strong-flying, parasitic, insect-eating birds, they have melodious voices —the well-known cuckoo clock, so beloved by children, is an imitation of the notes of the European cuckoo. The scientific name of the Common Cuckoo of Europe, *Cuculus canorus,* means "melodious." A jay-sized bird looking rather like a small hawk, this bird has gray or brown upper parts, grayish lower parts with dusky bars. Whether because of its hawklike appearance or because of its parasitic habits, groups of small birds in Europe often attack the cuckoo when they find it near their nests. But as individuals, they are afraid to approach too close to this hawklike bird, and so it is able to lay its egg in their nest.

The Hawk Cuckoo, *Cuculus sparveroides,* seventeen inches long, is an Indo-Malayan bird that closely parallels the appearance of a hawk. Its camouflage is so convincing that the first of these birds we collected was actually in our possession before we discovered its real identity. Even the behavior of this cuckoo is hawklike—it perches on exposed limbs and flies about with all the self-assurance of a hawk, instead of slinking through underbrush as do most other cuckoos. Briefly described, the hawk cuckoo is brown above, white below, with brown bars and a brown chest.

Some of the smaller cuckoos are brilliantly colored. Thus, the Violet Cuckoo, *Chalcites xanthorhynchus,* of the Philippines, is pure violet above with the entire under parts barred with black and white. Not a whit less striking is the metallic-glistening green Emerald Cuckoo of Africa. Among the larger parasitic cuckoos we find some that lay their eggs in crow nests. The biggest of these birds, the Channel-bill, *Scythrops*, of the Australian region, is a gray bird the size of a raven. It has a very big bill.

## MALCOHAS—BIRDS WITH GAUDY BILLS

Malcohas, which include some of the most beautiful cuckoos, are most abundant in the African and Indo-Malayan regions. All build nests and rear their own young. Malcohas have a thick bill, broad wings, strong legs, a long tail, and a rather clucking voice. We sometimes see them in tall trees, but these birds are really partial to undergrowth, bushes, and dense grass fields where they hop about energetically. Two of the most unusual kinds of malcohas dwell side by side on Luzon Island in the Philippines, where we have observed them. The Scale-feathered Cuckoo, *Phoenicophaeus cumingi*, is a long-tailed, bluish-black magpie-like bird. On examining one of these cuckoos closely, we found that the feathers of the head end in curly black vanes of cellophane-like texture. The Scarlet-eyebrowed Cuckoo, *Phoenicophaeus superciliosus*, a relative, has straggly red eyebrows and a pea-green bill.

The American Black-billed and Yellow-billed Cuckoos, *Coccyzus*, are cousins of the malcohas. Another near relative is the Squirrel-tailed Cuckoo, *Piaya cayana*, the most familiar cuckoo in South America (north to Mexico). Famous for its inquisitive personality, this denizen of the undergrowth and forest edge is reddish, with the head and neck more cinnamon; the ring around the eye is blood red and naked, the tail has broad white tips.

## ANIS—THEY PREFER COMMUNAL LIVING

Anis are jay-sized cuckoos of South America, the West Indies, and tropical North America. They have high-pitched whining notes.

In Panama we were able to observe the Smooth-billed Ani, which favors grassy clearings and orchards, often near water. These birds have a marked taste for communal living. They usually travel in flocks of from six to fourteen birds. When approached, they flap slowly and clumsily from bush to bush. At night they roost in tight knots in high bushes. The birds build a communal nest in which the females deposit a number of eggs—twenty-six is the known

[9-1]

The "plain turkey" of Australia is the only one of 23 species of bustards native to that continent; several species are found in Asia but the bulk of the family is concentrated in Africa. Bustards in general have heavier bodies and shorter legs than cranes and favor dry plains regions. They are swift runners and, weighing up to 30 pounds or more, are among the heaviest of flying birds.

[9-1A]

The only Australian member of the crane family proper is the five-foot brolga, commonly called the "Native Companion" because the bushmen often have a tame one in their camps. While the larger birds for the most part can be divided into either vegetarian or carnivorous types, cranes are more or less omnivorous, feeding equally well on grains, grasses, insects, amphibians and small mammals.

[9-1B]

The clapper rail is a typical American representative of the world-wide 132-specied family of running birds known as Rallidae. With long legs and toes and slender bodies ("thin as a rail") these excellent and elusive game birds slip swiftly through the dense vegetation of their salt marsh homes. Young clappers, like most rails, can run and swim almost as soon as they are hatched. Usually small-winged birds, rails take flight only as a last resort, although some species do make long migratory flights at night and others, dwelling on isolated islands, are completely flightless.

[9-2]

The smaller, shorter-billed sora rail is also a salt marsh dweller and like the clapper is most effectively hunted by flushing at high tide when the birds are forced to take wing. Most of the species live in fresh water areas and although they are as reluctant to take to the water as to the air, once in the water they are good swimmers and divers.

[9-2A]

The purple gallinule with its crimson beak is native to the warmer parts of the Western Hemisphere. Slightly larger than the rails and far more prone to fly and swim, gallinules favor fresh water ponds choked with water plants. "Gallinule" comes almost directly from the Latin diminutive for "hen" and European gallinules are known as "water hens" or "moor hens."

[9-2B]

The sandpiper family, with 77 species mostly spread over the northern portion of the Northern Hemisphere, is the largest group of shore birds and is named without any strain on the imagination: the birds live, with few exceptions, on sandy beaches and have a piping cry. The small (eight inches) spotted sandpiper loses its spots before migrating south in the fall; a change to simpler winter plumage is common among sandpipers.

[9-2C]

The jacksnipe is very closely related to the woodcock and is about the same size—12 inches. An equally desirable table delicacy, the snipe prefers open marshes or wet meadows while the woodcock sticks to the alder bogs, one of the few sandpipers that never visit the shore. Both are solitary birds, well distributed throughout the United States, and like all sandpipers are strong fliers.

[9-3]

Curlews are the longer-legged, heavier-bodied sandpipers with long, slender downwardly curved bills. While most sandpipers nest in the Arctic, they are among the last migrants to go north and the first to leave at the approach of cold weather. One variety of curlew nests in a desolate region of Alaska during the short northern summer, and spends the rest of the year in the Hawaiian Islands.

[9-3A]

The ruddy turnstone is regarded as a link between the plovers and sandpipers but because of its shorter legs and bill it is generally classified with the plovers ("rain birds" from their habit of scolding before rain). Technically shore birds but equally at home on coasts, plains or fields, the plover family is found in almost all parts of the world, their remarkable nonstop migratory journeys carrying them — in the case of the ruddy turnstone at least — almost from pole to pole.

[9-3B]

Although hunters have completely eradicated the American avocet east of the Mississippi, the handsome long-legged shore bird with its upwardly curved bill is still plentiful around the alkali lakes of western North America. The even longer-legged member of this small group of birds with upturned bills, the stilt, is often seen nesting with avocets but in contrast with the "localized" avocet population, stilts are found in all the warmer regions throughout the world.

[9-3C]

Wilson's phalarope nests in the marshes in the interior of North America while the other two species of this extremely odd family nest in the Arctic regions of both hemispheres. Near-kin to the shore birds, flocks of phalaropes numbering in the tens of thousands remain at sea for months, weathering all sorts of storms, seldom coming ashore except at nesting time. The female assumes the bright plumage and is the dominant partner at mating time, and the male is left to incubate the eggs and care for the young.

[9-4]

Terns are smaller than the true gulls, with more slender bills and weaker feet. Most species are white with black caps, gray mantles and forked tails, and are exceptionally graceful in flight. While they feed mainly by diving for small fish, the advent of the 17-year locust draws large flocks into wooded areas during the day; they return to the water at night.

[9-4A]

Distinguished from other birds by the vertical slitlike pupils of their eyes and their vertically flattened knifelike bill, the skimmer family consists of three species — one in Africa, one in India, and the American black skimmer which frequents the east coast from Massachusetts to Argentina. Skimmers fly low enough to cleave the water with the larger lower part of the bill, seizing whatever small marine life they happen to contact.

[9-4B]

Murres lay a single, relatively huge egg on the bare ground. Because of its odd cone- or pear-shape, the egg can roll only in a small circle and any such haphazard movement apparently has no ill effect on the young bird. The closely related murres, auks and puffins are the Arctic equivalent of the penguins, the auks proper bearing the most resemblance to the much larger penguins, but the surviving members of this family can still fly. In search of food they also "fly" underwater with a wing motion very similar to that which propels them through air.

[9-5]

The six species of sizable, conspicuous shore birds known as oyster catchers or mussel pickers inhabit the seacoasts of most of the world and some of the larger rivers of the Eastern Hemisphere. Wading in shallow water, the bird quickly jabs its sharp-edged bill into the open shell of an oyster or clam injuring the mollusk in such a way that it cannot close the shell. The black oyster catcher is native to western North America, ranging as far north as Alaska.

[9-5A]

The gulls are another widespread clan, the majority of the species dwelling along European, Asiatic and American seacoasts and the remainder, usually smaller varieties, near large inland bodies of water. The wholesale slaughter of gulls for their feathers was stopped by law in the United States and Canada a number of years ago and the predatory herring gull has so increased in numbers that the authorities now destroy the eggs to control its population.

[9-5B]

There is no real difference between doves and pigeons although the smaller more gentle birds of this family are usually referred to as doves. The mourning or turtle dove is the only common species of the Northern United States and Canada since unrestrained mass-slaughter exterminated its slightly larger but quite similar cousin, the passenger pigeon. Various species in more or less exotic forms are known throughout the world; the long extinct dodo of the Indian Ocean islands was a monstrous, flightless pigeon.

[9-6]

Most of the 315 species of parrots dwell in the warmer and less accessible parts of the world although fossil discoveries indicate they once lived in Europe and nontropical Asia as well. The brilliantly colored, long-tailed macaws are natives of tropical America. All the species have the remarkable "yoke-toed" foot structure—the first and fourth toes extend backward, enabling the birds to use the foot as a hand for holding food or in walking and climbing.

[9-6A]

The sulphur-crested cockatoo of the New Guinea forests is a raucously noisy bird with a very wary, suspicious nature. The parrot family's most characteristic feature is the powerful, sharply hooked bill the lower half of which is shorter, more stocky and sharply upcurved. The birds are primarily vegetarian and the larger varieties have little difficulty cracking heavy-shelled nuts.

[9-7]

Ranging from Mexico to Argentina, the blunt-tailed green Amazona are perhaps the most famous of New World parrots and, with the African gray parrots, are the most gifted talkers of this loquacious family. (Individual birds differ in their abilities, of course.) In captivity many of the species will imitate human speech and domestic animal noises but in the wild state they do not imitate other birds or animals.

[9-7A]

The difference between parakeets and parrots is a matter of size, parakeets being at the small end of the range. Since modern antibiotics overcome the once deadly "parrot disease" (psittacosis from Psittaciformes, the order in which all parrots are classified) the ban on their importation into the United States has been lifted, and parakeets like these have gained wide acceptance as pets. They also can be taught to talk, especially the brightly-colored male, but their speech is more difficult to understand as it is very rapid and much higher pitched than that of the larger parrots.

[9-7B]

The great black cockatoos share the New Guinea homeland with their vociferous white counterparts and as they are no less clamorous, flocks of the two birds create a considerable uproar. While some macaws attain a length of three feet, some members of this bluish-black species are thought to be even larger. The tremendous crest over the partially naked cheeks makes the great black cockatoo particularly conspicuous.

[9-8]

The barn owls with their insatiable appetite for rats and mice are a great boon to man the world over for, although they prefer the warmer regions, they are one of the most cosmopolitan of bird species. Known in parts of the United States as monkey-faced owls because of their odd appearance, many of these owls make their homes in church steeples and towers as well as barns, while still others prefer the owl standby — a hollow tree.

[9-8A]

With a powerful bill, feet like grappling hooks and the very fierce disposition usually associated with birds of prey, the great horned owl is sometimes referred to as the "tiger" of the bird world. It has been known to make off with domestic cats and turkeys and, on occasion, will rout the eagles. The American great horned owl adapts itself very well to most environments, as does its larger cousin, the eagle owl of Europe and Asia. India and Africa also have varieties of this vicious predator.

[9-9]

The snowy owl of the Arctic is one of the few species that hunt by day, but with the very long days of the Arctic summer it does not have much choice. It feeds mainly on lemmings, arctic hares and grouse, and like many other birds that inhabit bitter cold regions permanently, its legs are densely clad in feathers right down to the toes.

[9-9A]

Perhaps the most familiar of North American owls is the screech owl which gets its name from its characteristic melancholy wail. With a maximum length of 10 inches, the small owl has been known to nest in abandoned bird-houses — as long as it has a snug day-time refuge it is not particularly concerned about its proximity to human habitation. Some screech owls are red and others are gray but the color variation is not connected with age or sex, or anything else that can be determined: it is simply the way they are.

[9-10]
The burrowing owl dwells in the unforested regions of the western part of North America, ranging from southern Canada to Guatemala and Panama. North of Kansas the birds usually migrate. About an inch smaller than the screech owls, burrowing owls live underground and while they can dig for themselves if they have to (and the ground is soft), they prefer to take over abandoned prairie dog, gopher and badger holes. Most active in the early hours of the morning and evening, the little owls spend the greater part of the day sitting by their burrows surveying their neighborhood.

[9-10A]

The still smaller saw-whet owl of the Northeast and Northwest lacks none of the predatory habits of the larger species although the size of its prey is somewhat limited. Unlike most birds, owls enjoy binocular vision, both the large luminous eyes facing forward. However, the eyeballs do not move in the sockets and owls must turn their heads to see— a handicap compensated for by the ability to turn the head sufficiently to permit the bird to look directly behind it.

**[9-11]**

The wingbeats of a hovering hummingbird number about 55 to the second, producing a whirring sound but dissolving into a blur as far as vision is concerned. Hummingbirds are found only in the Americas, ranging from Cape Horn to Alaska and from sea level to 16,000-foot altitudes in the Andes but of the 319 known species only the migratory ruby-throat appears regularly east of the Mississippi. The species is named for the sparkling, irridescent ruby-red throat of the adult male, but in females and wintering males the beautiful red feathers are white.

**[9-11A]**

The slender folded wings of this rufous humming bird of the Northwest seem to belie the tremendous speed attained by the birds in short flights and their amazing endurance in the air in general. The nests of all the species are very similar — plant "cotton" decorated with lichens laced together with spider webs; and all the females lay two and only two tiny white eggs in a clutch. As in many bird families, the young are fed by regurgitation, the exceptionally long, slender bills of the adults being most effective "medicine droppers" for the feeding of their unbelievably small off-spring.

**[9-11 B & C]**

Although the "why" may not be too apparent to the layman, scientists have good reasons for classifying some 70 species of odd birds with odder names in one family — the nightjars. (The "jar" here comes from the jarring or churring sounds made by one European species.) The best known American species of this group is the nighthawk — which is not a hawk and is often as active during the day as at night. Most nightjars lay their two speckled eggs directly on rocky or gravel-covered ground, and the nighthawk has made a singularly effective adaptation of this custom: it lays its eggs on the flat gravelled roofs of city buildings where, safe from almost everything but man, it has an excellent chance to raise its brood successfully.

[9-12]

While they bear considerable resemblance to the owls, the 12 species of frogmouths which inhabit the Oriental and Australian tropical regions are also nightjars. Unlike their equally wide-mouthed (but far more widespread) cousins the goatsuckers, which fly with mouth agape into swarms of insects, the rather sluggish frogmouths are content with what moths and insects they can catch hopping about among tree limbs.

[9-12 A & B]

An Australian kookaburra kills a snake by beating its head on a log and then apparently discusses its nice lunch with a companion. Largest and most unusual member of the kingfisher family, the kookaburra feeds on reptiles, crabs, large insects, mice, rats—anything but fish. The bird's cry is an abrupt, discordant laugh which compares favorably with that of the hyena in startling weirdness, and gives the kookaburra its other common name "laughing jackass."

The many Old World (and one New World) species of cuckoos that lay their eggs in the nests of other, often smaller, birds have given the whole family a bad name. The slender, dovelike yellow-billed cuckoo of North America builds its own nest and carefully tends its young. Parasitic or not, the numerous species of this world-wide group of birds perform a valuable service by devouring myriads of harmful insects. And the parasitic habits of the bronzed cuckoo of the Southwest Pacific have given rise to the most baffling of all bird migrations: abandoned as eggs, hatched and raised by non-migratory foster parents, the fledglings unhesitatingly fly some 2,200 miles to join their parents.

[9-13A]

The woodpecker with its strong chisel-shaped bill, powerful neck muscles, modified head bones (to withstand the almost constant hammering), powerful feet with strong, sharply curved "yoke-toed" claws, and stiff pointed tail feathers with which to prop and balance itself, is remarkably well equipped for its rigorous life of drilling through solid hard wood for food and lodging. The more than 200 species have world-wide distribution, the largest of the better-known American species being the pileated woodpecker or logcock. The red crest should not lead to confusion with the redheaded woodpecker—the latter has a completely red head and large white wing patches, and is little more than half the size of the logcock.

[9-14]

The various species of flycatchers differ greatly in their nesting habits, the crested flycatchers of eastern North America, southwestern United States and tropical America preferring holes in trees, or reasonably accurate facsimiles. They have a habit of including castoff snakeskins in their nests, and some naturalists believe this is to scare away would-be robbers. Although not as brightly colored as some members of the family, the crested flycatchers have a loud mellow song which commands attention.

[9-14A]

Most swallows, entirely dependent on flying insects for food, are highly migratory but some tree swallows, hardier than most, winter as far north as Long Island, New York, ekeing out their diet with bayberries. Handsome birds, the tree swallows that do migrate present a remarkable sight when they gather by the thousand in marshes and on telephone wires before starting south. They nest usually in hollow tree stumps by ponds, and readily accept available bird houses.

[9-14B]

Even if the swallows did not perform such yeoman service in keeping down the insect population, they would still be welcome for the pleasure to be obtained from their graceful flight and soft musical twitterings. The "barn" swallow of the United States is the "common" swallow of the Old World and while these birds once nested exclusively on cliffs now almost invariably they make their homes on ledges and beams of barns and other buildings.

The rather plain little brown rough-winged swallow is one of the less sociable species, nesting singly in holes in gravel or river banks throughout most of the United States. It gets its name from the curious file-like projections on the leading edge of its wings. (Only the barn swallows have the deeply forked "swallow tail.")

[9-15A]

The largest and most conspicuous of American swallows is the purple martin. Extremely sociable, these birds thoroughly enjoy the large apartment type of birdhouses people build for them, but they will let the smaller, more aggressive English sparrows dispossess them.

[9-15B]

The brown thrasher is closely related to the mockingbird and is also an excellent songster, but it rarely mimics other birds as does its more drab gray and white cousin. The handsome chestnut colored bird lives in the dense brush of the eastern United States, but two or three very similar species are found from the southwestern desert areas down into Mexico.

[9-16]

The catbird which resembles the mockingbird in appearance is more closely related to the thrashers, but its petulant scolding cry is a grating travesty of the songs of the other two species. It ranges farther north than the mockingbird and farther west than the brown thrasher, but has many of the thrashers habits in general. The cup-shaped nest in dense foliage is typical of the family — the wide-open mouths greeting a seemingly weary parent are all too typical of baby-bird world.

record—and incubate in a group. One nest we found was three feet up in a thick bush beside water. At the time of our discovery it contained two white eggs—later devoured by an iguana.

## GROUND CUCKOOS

**The Road Runner,** *Geococcyx,* the best-known member of this group, dwells in the deserts of southwestern North America. It is a very unusual bird, with such nicknames as "snake-eater," "war bird," "cock-of-the-desert," and "lizard bird." This brownish cuckoo has a spotted crest, and its bright eyes give it an alert look. Its strong legs enable it to run like a deer, and for a goodly distance; it takes to flying only as a last resort.

THE "SNAKE-EATER"

This is one of the many names for the road runner, a cuckoo that is famous for its ability to kill rattlesnakes. The bird, which dwells in the American Southwest and Mexico, runs with dashing, headlong swiftness. The road runner's favorite food is lizards, but it also eats snails after smashing them against rocks.

The road runner's great claim to fame is its prowess in killing rattlesnakes. Apparently the rattler's venom, coils, and rattles hold no terrors for the road runner. The film *The Adventures of Chico* pictures the exciting duel between these two creatures and thus enables us to appreciate the remarkable deftness and uncanny timing of the road runner. Managing by rapid movements to stay just out of reach of the terrible fangs, the bird exasperates its opponent by stabbing it with its beak. The road runner approaches when the snake is uncoiled and hence not poised for a thrust; or the bird changes the direction of approach, causing the snake to turn laboriously. Finally, worn out by the struggle, the rattler admits defeat and tries to make off. The road runner, with victory in sight, seizes the snake at the back of the head, and shakes it and waves it viciously and pounds it on the ground. At last the snake is vanquished, and the road runner swallows it, starting with the head.

A road runner has been seen with part of a two-foot snake dangling from the bird's mouth. One observer reported seeing a road runner vanquish a rattlesnake three and one-half feet long. According to this account, the struggle ended when the bird punctured the rattler's brain by a powerful thrust of its beak through the snake's skull; the road runner, so we are told, ate the brain but drew the line at that point. There is a legend in the Southwest to the effect that the road runner makes a practice of building corrals of cactus spines around sleeping rattlers.

The road runner's favorite food is lizards, and it feeds small ones to its young almost right after hatching. Amusingly enough, the chicks eat the lizards head first, and it is not uncommon to see the tail of a lizard hanging out of the chick's mouth. The road runner is also fond of land snails; it smashes their shells against rocks by appropriate movements of its neck and beak.

The road runner builds a nest in a cactus bush and lays white eggs.

### COUCALS—THROWBACKS TO A PAST AGE

The coucals of the Old World are very strange birds. There is something so primitive about them that they would not have appeared out of place in a Jurassic swamp with *Archaeopteryx,* some 125 million years ago.

In the typical coucal the claw of the hind toe is long and straight, and the bill rather straight and thick; the legs are long and strong, the feathers of the head and chest stiff·and pointed. The plumage is generally blackish, buffy, or brownish. Coucals rear their own young in a domed nest which has a side entrance and is always placed near the ground.

The Pheasant Coucal, *Centropus phasianinus,* of New Guinea and Australia, is larger than a crow but more slender. It has stiff, spiny feathers—in flight it is ungainly—but its long powerful legs are admirably suited for life on the ground. We often observed the pheasant coucal in kunai grass fields among bushes and boulders. It is a blackish-brown bird with narrow buff streaks and close reddish barring. When flushed from grass it often perches clumsily on low bushes, where, frequently, because of its ungainly proportions, it more resembles a dead limb than a bird.

## TURACOS OR PLANTAIN EATERS— BEAUTIFUL BIRDS OF AFRICA

Making their home only in Africa, the twenty or so kinds of turacos are among the most unusual and beautiful birds of that continent. Long-tailed birds of pigeon size or larger, turacos live entirely among trees, running along the limbs with all the agility of a squirrel. In the African forests where these birds are at home, the loud resonant calls of turacos are heard almost constantly. They feed chiefly on wild fruits, varying their fare with green leaves and an occasional snail or insect. The belief that these birds eat plantains (bananas) is apparently erroneous—hence the native name *turaco* is preferable to "plantain eaters."

The turaco's nest is a frail platform of sticks. The bird lays two or three white, bluish, or greenish eggs. Though naturalists usually place the turacos with the cuckoos in the order Cuculiformes, there are certain similarities between the turaco family (Musophagidae) and the gallinaceous (fowl-like) birds.

A typical turaco—the South African Lourie, *Turacus corythaix,* for example—has dense silky green plumage becoming glossy bluish on the wings and tail. A handsome, erect, white-bordered green crest adorns its head; the eye is set off by a circlet of white feathers. The wing quills are a deep rich maroon which we can see only when the bird is flying or spreading its wings. This brilliant color is produced by turacin, a pigment that contains copper and is present in no other family of birds. Formerly naturalists believed that this red pigment, possessed by all but a very few turacos, was washed out by rain; but this seems to happen very rarely.

**THE TURACO—A UNIQUE AFRICAN BIRD**
Turacos are among Africa's loveliest birds. Many have wing feathers of a deep, rich maroon that is produced by a pigment known as "turacin." No other bird secretes this substance. As it runs along tree branches with all the agility of a squirrel, the turaco calls with loud, resonant notes. Shown here is the blue turaco.

The Violet Turaco, *Musophaga violacea,* lacks the harmonizing colors of the South African lourie. A purple, somewhat gaudy-looking bird, it has a maroon crest and the usual red wing patches. The large yellow bill extends onto the forehead as a bony casque.

An Abyssinian turaco, *Corythaixoides,* called the "Go-away Bird" from its note, is quite unlike other members of the family when it comes to color. Its back and breast are gray, the abdomen white, and the wing and tail feathers black banded with white.

By far the largest member of the family is the Blue Turaco, *Corytheola.* Some three feet long, it is one of the most conspicuous and noisy birds of the African forest, where it occurs in bands of half a dozen. When flying, it takes a few leisurely wingbeats and then sails for some distance. It has blue plumage, washed with green on the breast and reddish on the abdomen. The large, pompon-like crest is black.

# Owls—Creatures of the Night

SINCE FAR BACK in the dim past, men have associated the owl with the black arts, and with wisdom and grave learning. If you are familiar with some of the exquisite coins of the ancient Greek city-states, you have probably seen their representation of the goddess Athene and her owl. Just as Athene was the goddess of wisdom, the owl was the symbol of wisdom. To the Romans, who called this goddess Minerva, the owl was "Minerva's bird." In the Middle Ages there appeared in England an allegorical work, *The Owl and the Nightingale,* in which an owl, representing the clergy, debated with a nightingale, representing the nobility. Today the owl maintains its literary stronghold in "The Owl and the Pussycat." Yet there still remains an aura of mystery about the owl, even though we are aware that what once passed for inscrutability may be nothing more than lethargy.

To begin with, we are all familiar with the eerie sounds the owl utters—hoots, screeches, or wails, which may well have filled people of earlier times with a feeling of superstitious awe. This was all the more likely since owls are nighttime creatures—few of them hunt by day. Add to this the fact that owls are birds of prey, and grimly efficient ones at that. For a long time naturalists associated the owls with the hawks, but the experts came to realize that the resemblance between these birds extends only to their fitness for preying on other birds and small mammals. Actually owls (they make up the order Strigiformes) are related to that other group of nighttime birds, the queerly named nightjars or goatsuckers.

## POWERFUL BIRDS OF PREY

As birds of prey, owls have one great advantage over hawks. Where these latter swoop down with noisy whirrs of their powerful pinions, the owls make the same deadly descent in complete silence, as their feathers are fringed with down. No wonder the owl is sure death for rodents, shrews, and other small mammals that are abroad at night. From man's point of view, owls are among the most valuable of all our birds, for they are famous destroyers of harmful rodents and insects. When devouring a victim, owls generally swallow mice or other small prey whole. In due course they regurgitate fur and indigestible bones in the form of pellets. These are sometimes found in large numbers at owl roosts and, when studied carefully, they yield valuable information about what owls feed on.

Since the owl is active at night and since it is a bird of prey, you would not expect its plumage to be bright—and it isn't. But whatever owls lack in the way of brilliant coloring, they make up for it in subtle shading and intricacy of feather pattern. Their eyes, too, are adapted for nightlife and stealthy prowling. Their eyes are very large—one of the features that give owls an "owlish" appearance—to enable them to make the most of the weak light available at night.

Owls also differ from most birds in that both their eyes face forward, giving them binocular vision; other birds must scrutinize an object with only one eye at a time. The owl seems to enjoy an advantage, too, as regards hearing. Although no birds have a true external ear, the feathers surrounding the ear openings of owls are often thin and bristle-like—perhaps to permit better penetration by sound waves. We find also that in some owls the ear openings themselves are much larger than in other birds.

As we have noted in the case of many birds of prey, the female owl is larger than her mate. Most owls nest in hollow trees or other natural cavities and lay white eggs. These eggs are rounder than most birds'—probably an adaptation that makes it easier for the incubating bird to turn the eggs in such close quarters as are provided in a tree cavity. Some owls, you may recall, are pugnacious enough to usurp the nest of an eagle. They sometimes mete out the same disrespectful treatment to a crow or hawk. Young owls are covered with down, and grow rather slowly to maturity despite their tremendous appetites.

## SCREECH OWLS

**The Screech Owl,** *Otus asio,* is perhaps the most familiar owl in North America. A small bird with a maximum length of ten inches or so, it has a characteristic melancholy cry that accounts for its name. We encounter the screech owl wherever it has managed to find a hollow tree—even in a village—that affords it refuge during the day and a place to nest. Like many other owls, the screech owl has two earlike tufts of feathers on its forehead. This bird has two color varieties—some individuals are gray, others reddish brown. These color distinctions have nothing to do with sex or age—you may find gray and brown young in a single brood.

## GREAT HORNED OWLS—FIERCE YET WARY BIRDS

**The Great Horned Owl,** *Bubo virginianus,* is sometimes dubbed the "tiger" of the bird world. The most powerful of all the owls, it is also one of the largest, with a length of twenty-three inches or thereabouts. Aside from the absence of the reddish-brown coloring, the great horned owl might pass for a giant-size version of the screech owl. Feeding on rabbits, rats, and almost any other medium-sized prey it can find, this ferocious owl disposes every now and then of a domestic cat, a hen, or a skunk. It has been known to seize turkeys on their night roost and to drive off eagles. Its bill is powerful, its feet like grappling hooks.

This owl has just the kind of very fierce disposition that we associate with birds of prey. Its young, even when taken from the nest at an early age, usually prove vicious and intractable. As with most owls, the female is considerably larger than her mate. Her hooting differs in pitch from the male's, so that you can distinguish the pair as they answer one another.

For all its great size and sometimes destructive food habits, the great horned owl is a wary creature. Holding its own better than most owls, it is a long-lived bird, and one great horned owl reached the age of sixty-eight years in a zoo. Of course, such an age is not indicative for life in the wild. Still, as you might expect from these traits, this owl is very adaptable, and gets along just as well in the deserts of Arizona as in the great Canadian forests. Like most other owls, it does not migrate; it does happen occasionally that some individuals move south when faced with a shortage of food.

In Europe and Asia we find a cousin of the great horned owl, but even larger—the Eagle Owl, *Bubo maximus* ("the biggest"). Other species make their home in India and Africa.

**A FIERCE BIRD OF PREY**

The great horned owl is so fierce that it has been known to drive eagles from their nests. Preying on fowl and small mammals, it seizes them with talons that have been likened to grappling hooks. Like other owls, it is able to descend in absolute silence on its victims because its downy plumage muffles any sound that might be produced in flight. A long-lived bird, the great horned owl is highly adaptable to extremes of climate.

## BARRED OWLS—CANNIBALS ON OCCASION

**The Barred Owl**, *Strix varia*, feeds chiefly on mice, frogs, and similar small prey. Not infrequently it makes a meal of its smaller cousin the screech owl. You can readily distinguish the barred owl's hoot, which ends in a wailing squall. This owl does not have ear tufts, and it also differs from most other owls in having brown—not yellow—eyes. Widely distributed throughout eastern North America, the barred owl has a cousin, the Spotted Owl, *Strix maculosa,* a rare bird found locally on the Pacific seaboard.

Another cousin of the barred owl is the Great Gray Owl or Lapland Owl, *Strix nebulosa,* which dwells in the heavy cone-bearing forests of the Northern Hemisphere, and occasionally as far south as Maine. Although it is a beautiful owl and very large—about thirty-three inches long—it is actually a huge ball of feathers, quite inferior to the great horned owl in strength and weight.

## SNOWY OWLS OF THE ARCTIC

**The Snowy Owl or White Owl,** *Nyctea scandiaca,* is well known to us, if only in pictures. It is one of the few owls that hunt by day—it has no choice during the long Arctic summer on the tundras where it nests. Normally it feeds on lemmings and on arctic hares and grouse. To withstand the rigors of the northern winter, this owl of the Arctic is densely clad in feathers right down to its toes.

## SHORT-EARED OWLS—THEY MIGRATE MORE THAN MOST

As we have seen, owls are not much given to migrating. The Short-eared Owl, *Asio flammeus,* is an exception. Perhaps because of its willingness to undertake long flights it was able to establish itself even in the Hawaiian Islands. This owl lives mainly in marshes or wasteland, and mice are its favorite food. It lays five or six eggs and, like most owls, begins incubating as soon as the first egg is laid. The result is that the young hatch out over a period of several days and vary quite a bit in size and development.

## ELF OWLS OF THE DESERT

Some species of owls are no bigger than a sparrow; one of the most interesting of these is the cute little Elf Owl, *Micrathene whitneyi,* no more than six inches long. Dwelling in the American Southwest, it usually sets up housekeeping in a giant cactus. Often you may see its round little head as it peers about in the entrance to its home. Like most small owls, the elf owl lives mainly on insects. Each pair seem to have their own hunting territory, and a resident owl will be quick to challenge an intruder if he whistles an imitation of its notes.

## BARN OWLS—PARTICULARLY USEFUL TO MAN

**The Barn Owl,** *Tyto alba,* devours tremendous numbers of rats and mice. This voracious appetite is a boon so far as man is concerned. About eighteen inches long, the bird has such a queer appearance that it is known as the Monkey-faced Owl in many parts of the United States. Look at the owl closely and you will see that its plumage reveals beautifully mottled shades of buff and brown.

A greedy eater, as we have noted, the barn owl is admirably equipped for keeping itself well fed. The tendons of its legs, as in other birds of prey, are attached to the bones in such a way that they automatically close the claws in a tight grip when the leg is bent. And so, as the bird makes contact with its prey after swooping down with legs outstretched, its weight causes its legs to bend, whereupon the talons tighten and pierce the vitals of the unfortunate rat or mouse. This adaptation is merely a further refinement of one found in many birds which makes it possible for them to automatically grasp a perch while sleeping at night.

Though partial to warmer regions, the barn owl is one of the most cosmopolitan of birds and is found throughout the world—even such out-of-the-way spots as the Fiji Islands. These owls frequently make their homes in church steeples, towers, or barns; many, however, still prefer hollow trees. The barn owls have cousins in the Old World, particularly in the Australian region. They all share with the common barn owl certain peculiarities of body structure that may justify naturalists in placing them in a family distinct from the other owls.

# Goatsuckers and Their Relatives

I**N THIS GROUP** we find some queer birds—and queerer names. Goatsuckers do not suck the milk of goats. Nighthawks are not hawks and are fairly active in the daytime. Whippoorwills are named after their famous cry, as are chuck-will's-widows. Nightjars are named for the curious jarring quality of their notes. The potoos and frogmouths are chiefly remarkable for their wide, capacious mouths. Oilbirds, once valuable for their body grease, live a batlike existence. Strangest of all the members of this order (the Caprimulgiformes) is the Poorwill, the only bird definitely known to hibernate!

## GOATSUCKERS OR NIGHTJARS—THE BIGMOUTHS

Where does the name "goatsuckers" come from? It seems to date back to Aristotle's statement that these birds use their huge mouths to suck milk from goats. There is no basis whatever for this belief —the true function of this wide gap is to engulf night-flying insects. In fact, it is not uncommon for one of these birds to fly, mouth agape, right into a swarm of insects. Large bristles extending from the corners of the mouth help rake them in.

A better name for the seventy species of this family (the Caprimulgidae) is "nightjars." The word "jar" derives here from the "jarring" notes—akin to the churring of a wheel—of the European Nightjar, *Caprimulgus europaeus.* Several American goatsuckers also have names that are really renderings of their loud calls. Among these are the Poorwill, *Phalaenoptilus nuttalli,* and, as we have seen, the Whippoorwill, *Caprimulgus vociferus,* and the Chuck-will's-widow, *Caprimulgus carolinus.*

Like the owls, to whom they are related, nightjars are usually

1061

active only at night, spending the day perched unobtrusively on the ground or on the limb of a tree. Their feet are weak—so much so that they usually lie lengthwise on a limb for added support. Nightjars often make good use of protective coloration. Their plumage, for example, has a beautifully intricate and blending pattern which camouflages them to perfection when they are at rest.

## NIGHTHAWKS—FINE FLIERS BUT NOT HAWKS

**The Nighthawk,** *Chordeiles minor,* despite its name, has no relation to the true hawks. Unlike most of its cousins, it is partial to open country and is often active by day as well as by night. For these reasons, and also because it is the most generally distributed of the tribe, it is the best known of American nightjars. With a wingspread of about eighteen inches, it is a conspicuous bird as it swoops tirelessly, albeit somewhat erratically, through the air—usually at a considerable elevation. At courtship time the male attracts attention by a spectacular dive earthward—then checking its descent so quickly that the rush of air through its wing quills produces a loud booming noise. The nighthawk's long narrow wings are marked with a white spot. Its characteristic call is a loud, nasal *peent.*

Like most of its fellow nightjars, the nighthawk does not bother to build a nest; it simply lays its two eggs directly on the ground in a rocky or gravel-covered spot. Mottled with gray, the eggs are hard to see. Later on, the downy young also match their surroundings closely. One of the most remarkable traits of nighthawks is their habit of laying their eggs on the gravel-covered flat roofs of city buildings. This has advantages, if only to keep the eggs safe from such marauders as egg-eating snakes. If undisturbed by man, the birds frequently succeed in raising their young on top of the buildings.

Nightjars live almost entirely upon flying insects and, as you might expect, the members of the family that normally dwell in temperate regions migrate to the tropics with the coming of cold weather. This of course applies to the nighthawk, and you may sometimes see vast numbers of them heading south by day—though the other kinds travel by night. In the latter event, the birds rest during the day, waiting for the approach of twilight, when they can devour the insects that appear in full force at that time.

## TWO NIGHT BIRDS AND A HIBERNATING BIRD

The shy whippoorwill is the best known bird of the night in many forested parts of the United States. Though it is rarely seen—except as a shadow flitting through the twilight—its presence is immediately revealed to you by its loud cries. Over and over again it utters its call with breathless haste. On one occasion John Burroughs counted no less than 390 consecutive calls by one bird. The whippoorwill puts its nocturnal wanderings to good use—it is a great insect-destroyer. Its cousin the chuck-will's-widow is an equally noisy bird, though it favors more southerly regions. About the size of a pigeon, the "widow" has such a wide mouth that it sometimes swallows warblers, sparrows, and other small birds at night, doubtless mistaking them for insects.

**A NIGHT BIRD NAMED FOR ITS FAMOUS CALL**

Heard but not seen, the whippoorwill is famous for its characteristic call in the night. It repeats this call over and over—a naturalist counted some four hundred consecutive calls. The whippoorwill eats great quantities of insects during its nightly wanderings.

Naturalists made one of the most remarkable discoveries of recent years when they verified that the poorwill, which dwells in western North America, sometimes spends the winter in hibernation. For three successive winters they found one of these birds in the same rocky niche on a canyon wall in the Chuckawalla Mountains of California. During the hibernating period they were able to handle it freely without disturbing it—even the beam of a small flashlight failed to evoke a response when shone directly into its half-open eyes. Their astonishment at its torpid behavior faded when they found that this poorwill's temperature was in the neighborhood of 65° Fahrenheit. As we have seen earlier, slightly over 100° is normal for birds.

## POTOOS—THEIR MOUTHS CAN CLOSE OVER A TENNIS BALL

The Giant Potoos or Wood Nightjars of the New World tropics are owl-like birds of the night with mouths huge enough to be capable of closing over a tennis ball.

Potoos may sometimes be seen at dusk gliding over grassy savannas, but it is more usual to find them after dark when their large bulging eyes cast golden reflections in the beam of a torch. In our wanderings at night we have come on solitary birds perched on a fence post or on a rock outcropping in a forest clearing. In Panama we heard the mournful wail, "Poor—me—one" of a potoo (*Nyctibius griseus*) almost every night of the dry season. After dark, potoos foray out flycatcher-like from selected perches in quest of large night-flying insects. The potoos are grouped in the family Nyctibiidae.

The potoo's nest is a slight hollow on the top of a post or in the side of a decaying tree, anywhere from four to twenty feet above the ground. Here the female deposits a single white egg marked with violet and brown. It takes some seventy days to incubate the eggs and care for the young. The way the incubating adult projects from the sides of the nest stub makes the bird appear to be merely an extension of the limb or post.

The Great Potoo, *Nyctibius grandis,* of tropical America, is about the size of a large slender owl. Its plumage is marked with wavy dark brown lines, the abdomen is whitish. The downy, barred young is most remarkable, its broad head resembling a puppy's.

## OILBIRDS—CAVE DWELLERS BY DAY

The oilbird or guacharo is a curious bird which makes up a family all by itself, though in some ways it is like the owls and goatsuckers. Oilbirds live in huge colonies in tropical countries, clustering like bats in dark cave recesses by day and foraging far afield at night in great, croaking flocks in search of fruit. They are much sought after by the natives, who provide themselves with illumination and a butter-substitute by killing the birds and melting them down for their body grease.

The oilbird is the only member of the family Steatornithidae. It was the famous naturalist Alexander von Humboldt who discovered this bird in Venezuelan coastal caves in 1799 on a scientific expedition with Aimée Bonpland. More recently, naturalists have come across the birds in isolated caves on Trinidad, in the Guianas, and in the Andes of Colombia, Ecuador, and Peru.

About eighteen inches long, the oilbird has reddish-brown plumage, with oval whitish spots on its wings. Its sharply hooked bill is ringed with stiff bristles. The oilbird builds a platform of dried mud for its nest, and lays two to four white eggs which are spotted with reddish brown.

## OWLET FROGMOUTHS

We find the few species of owlet frogmouths in Australia and New Guinea. Making up the family Aegothelidae, they nest in hollow trees and sit upright like owls—traits that place them between the owls and the more typical nightjars or goatsuckers.

## FROGMOUTHS—THEY HAVE AN ENORMOUS GAPE

Frogmouths, as we have seen, get their common name from their enormous gape. The resemblance to a frog is enhanced by the broad, flat bill. Rather sluggish, inactive birds, they hop about among tree limbs seizing moths or large insects, instead of feeding on the wing like most of their relatives. There are a dozen species of frogmouths, grouped in the family Podargidae, and they make their home in the Oriental and Australian areas of the Old World tropics.

Some frogmouths are as large as a good-sized owl, and they are akin to owls in their habit of sleeping upright on a tree limb during the day. Frogmouths are also about the size of the potoos of the American tropics, and somewhat similar to them in appearance. Unlike other nightjars, the frogmouths build a nest of twigs in a tree. It is a flimsy structure, barely sturdy enough to support the eggs and young.

# Swifts and Hummingbirds

T HESE ARE among the smallest birds, and also among the most remarkable. Some of the swifts are generally accorded the distinction of being the fastest of all flying birds, while the hummingbirds have so many entrancing aspects that it would not be easy to single out one special feature. What is most astonishing about them, perhaps, is the endless variety of their lovely color schemes. The classification of the swifts and hummingbirds has been a matter of much discussion among naturalists. In this book these birds are grouped in the order Apodiformes.

## SWIFTS—THE MOST ENERGETIC OF ALL THE BIRDS

Swifts are just that: swift. About five inches long on the average, these small birds are capable of fifty-five miles an hour—and more. Naturalists believe that the larger swifts are the fastest fliers of all the birds, rivaled only by some of the bigger falcons. Living in groups, many of the seventy-eight species of swifts—all told, they make up the family Apodidae—travel in droves that spiral skillfully across the horizon. Their flight is jerky, interspersed with long glides, and they often indulge in such aerial antics as changing formation in midair. Fleet of wing as they are and seemingly tireless, swifts are the most energetic of all birds on the wing.

Do not think, however, that the swift's extraordinary flying abilities are its chief claim to fame. It is unique among birds because it never perches on horizontal surfaces. The swift's feet are too weak to support the weight of its body. Swifts, then, are able to rest only when they are clinging to vertical surfaces. Away from these, all their contacts with food, drink, and with each other must necessarily be made while in full flight! Living on insects which they catch on the

1066

wing—naturally—swifts suffer grievously in periods of prolonged storms when flying insects are not available. Both young and adult swifts have been known to perish in great numbers at such times.

Even when swifts gather nesting material, they assemble it on the wing. They snatch floating plant cotton from the air or else they tear or break free bits of grass or twigs as they fly past. Thus, the familiar Chimney Swift, *Chaetura pelagica,* of North America, grabs brittle twigs with its tiny feet while in full flight. Often a bird attacks a single twig repeatedly until it finally succeeds in breaking it loose. Then it glues the material to a vertical surface in some dark spot— usually the inside of an unused chimney or a hollow tree. The half-saucer nest may be near the top or as much as twenty feet deep in the cavity. The chimney swift has sharp claws and spiny tail feathers to help it cling to the interior of a tree or chimney.

Swifts live all over the world, and those of the temperate zones are migratory. They range from the size of small swallows (with which they are often confused) to that of a small falcon. The swift has a very small bill, but the broad gape is effectively adapted for engulfing flying insects. The large salivary glands produce an exceptionally sticky saliva used in nest-building. Robust and streamlined, the swift's body is cloaked with hard, glossy, greenish-black or dark-brown plumage. A few species have brighter feathers—chestnut or white collars, for example. Without exception the female resembles the male and the young assume the adult plumage as soon as they shed their down.

The famous Chinese penchant for "bird's nest soup," of which you have probably heard, had its origin in the nesting habits of the little cave-swiftlets of the Indo-Australian region. Perhaps the most peculiar of all swifts, these birds like to live in colonies, and they all use glutinous saliva in constructing their nests; at least one, *Collocalia inexpectata,* fashions the entire basket with it. This is how the Chinese harvest the nests: Shortly before the breeding season starts, they sweep out all the old nests from the cave walls. As soon as new nests have been constructed, they are harvested. This may be done repeatedly in the early stage of the breeding season, but in due course the swifts are allowed to breed in peace. Thus, the colony is not depleted. As with all swifts, the eggs are pure white and oval shaped, and the young are born naked.

The swift has a high-pitched, twittering voice; some species are very shrill. The Collared Swift of Central and South America, *Streptoprocne zonaris,* can be heard a hundred yards away when the wind is right. We were once attracted by the strange calls of these birds to a waterfall situated four thousand feet up in a spur of the eastern Andes of Colombia. As we watched at dusk, we saw collared swifts fly through the spray at the edge of the falls and disappear behind them. Famous for their habit of roosting and nesting under roaring waterfalls, the collared swifts have a wingspread of eighteen inches and are blackish except for a prominent white collar.

**FAST AND NOISY**
The collared swift is one of the largest of all the swifts—birds credited with being the fastest fliers of all. It is seen in flocks near waterfalls. Under the right conditions its shrill voice carries about a hundred yards. Note the conspicuous white collar.

Familiar as the chimney swift is to us, it remained until recently one of the great mysteries of nature. Literally millions of these birds enter and leave North America every year. So large are these migrating flocks that thousands of the birds have been trapped in a single night for banding and study. Yet, until recently they disappeared across our southern borders—not to be seen until spring, when, invariably, they winged their way northward right on schedule. At last, chimney-dwelling swifts were observed on the middle Amazon in March and some of them were seen in upper Amazonia. Thus naturalists have at least partially solved the mystery of the chimney swift's winter quarters.

## CRESTED, OR TREE, SWIFTS

Tree swifts differ from true swifts in a number of ways. The chief distinction is that their legs are much larger and stronger, enabling them to perch like normal birds. What confirms the tree swifts' kinship to the swifts is their habit of glueing their small cup-shaped nest to its anchorage on the side of a limb high on a forest tree and then securing the single egg to the inside of the nest with saliva.

The three species of tree swifts—they compose the family Hemiprocnidae—range from India and the Philippines to the Solomon Islands. They include the Whiskered Tree Swift, *Hemiprocne mystacea,* of Malaya and the Australian region. Fully a foot long, this bird has long narrow wings and a long but very slender forked tail. Its head is black, with lines of projecting white feathers on the face— hence the name "whiskered."

In New Guinea we occasionally found small parties of these birds in the deep forest. Again and again they would return to their high perches, even after being scared off by gunfire.

## HUMMINGBIRDS—INCREDIBLY SMALL, INCREDIBLY BEAUTIFUL

Hummingbirds are so beautiful that in the opinion of some naturalists they surpass even the peacock and bird of paradise in loveliness of appearance. Whether or not you share that view, you will find that these "glittering gems" of the bird world are truly among Nature's wonders. The smallest hummingbird, about two inches long and weighing in the neighborhood of one-tenth of an ounce, is the smallest of all feathered creatures. It lays two unbelievably tiny white eggs in a nest no bigger than a walnut shell. Even the Giant Hummingbird is only a "giant" by comparison, with its mere nine-inch length.

Yet this little bird is admirably equipped for superbly precise flying. Its name gives you a hint of its prowess—the wings move so rapidly that they produce a whirring sound; and their motion, as far as our vision is concerned, is nothing but a blur. The whirring is most noticeable when hummers hover to feed on nectar-laden flowers. At such times, the bird's wingbeats are about fifty-five to the second, and to photograph it you need an exposure of no more than one five-thousandth of a second.

Some hummingbirds make fairly long migrations, partly nonstop as when they cross bodies of water. Yet it is in brief flights that they are outstanding—perhaps the fastest flying birds on short hauls. Many species are capable of such remarkably swift movements that their darting flight reminds us of the passage of an arrow through the air. One moment the hummingbird is hovering close to the ground, hanging over a favorite flower extracting the sweet contents; the next moment it shoots to the very summit of a lofty tree—as if launched from a bow.

Of all the birds, only the hummingbird is capable of true backward flight. Its aerial maneuvering is remarkably similar to that employed by the modern twin-'coptered multi-place helicopters. However, while the twin blades of the man-made machine travel in horizontal paths, the wings of the hummingbird describe oval circles diagonal to the ground.

Hummingbirds dwell only in the Americas. We may find them at sea level or at an altitude of sixteen thousand feet in the equatorial Andes; some live near Cape Horn, others in Alaska. Certain species, as we have seen, are migrators. This is chiefly true of hummers in the temperate zones; the Ruby-throated Hummingbird, *Archilochus colubris,* of eastern North America, winters south to Panama. Still, others spend their whole lives in narrow floral belts hardly more than a few hundred yards in width; many are as effectively "rooted" as plants to the confines of a single mountain peak or little island.

It is in the subtropical zone of Colombia and Ecuador that hummingbirds are most plentiful. Of the 319 known species—all told, they make up the family Trochilidae—no less than 133 make their home in Colombia. Though we find eighteen species in the United States, only eight of these appear any distance to speak of from the Mexican border. In fact, only one, the ruby-throat, appears regularly east of the Mississippi.

The hummingbird's legs are weak and delicate. The wings are very strong in comparison—just what you would expect of a bird that spends most of its active hours aloft, feeding entirely on the wing with the aid of its highly specialized bill. There are cases where specialization reaches such a point of refinement that the bill is a good five inches long and is used with only one type of flower. Generally the bill has a slight downward curve and a sharp point; but in some cases it is nearly straight and in others it describes a circle-like curve.

To get at its favorite nectar, the hummingbird has developed a specialized tongue too; in fact, it is complex to a point matched by no other bird's tongue. The outer part of this tongue is rolled or tubular. At the throat it is linked to a fork in the hyoid (tongue) bones. The prongs of these bones pass under the throat and around the skull to anchorages on the forehead. With this extraordinary apparatus it becomes possible to take up the immense recoil of the long tongue; and so the hummingbird is able to reach deep into the innermost recesses of certain flowers and to extract nectar, tiny insects, and spiders. Because of their specialized feeding habits, hummingbirds are important pollinators of flowers—almost the only birds in the New World that play this typical insect-role.

Hummingbirds are active during the day, though it is true that we see many species only at dawn and dusk. And there are many others that live in twilight deep in the cathedral forests of the tropics, while still others dwell in the tops of the trees where they are even harder to discover. However, most of them are found in savannas of the lowlands and along the edge of open forests in areas where flowers are plentiful. In such places we are apt to find great numbers of hummingbirds together, creating the deceptive impression of a taste for group living. They have no flair for song, their best effort being a feeble cheep or squeak.

These birds are surprisingly fearless as far as man is concerned, and will readily venture in his presence. They are equally unafraid in facing any creature that approaches their nest. As for their methods of nest-building, the technique of the ruby-throated hummingbird is typical for the group. It fashions its nest of plant cotton and decorates it with lichens laced together with spider webs, usually saddling the structure on a small limb about twenty feet above the ground. It lays two tiny white eggs—this is true of the whole tribe. It takes about two weeks to hatch the young, blind and naked—yet in another three weeks they are feathered and ready to leave the nest. During the final days in the nest they grip the edge with their feet and flutter their wings to strengthen them for flight.

At courting time, male hummingbirds zoom through the air in spectacular dives. After mating, the females usually take on the whole responsibility for nest-building, incubating, and caring for the young. Some kinds of male hummers do, it is claimed, take an interest in family affairs. The females are efficient mothers. For example, the female Black-chinned Hummingbird, *Archilochus alexandrae,* gets no assistance from her mate. Yet she has been observed building a second nest and laying eggs in it, while she is still feeding her first pair in their nest.

**THE ONLY HUMMINGBIRD OF EASTERN NORTH AMERICA**
Hummingbirds generally live in the tropics. The only "hummer" that ventures into eastern North America is the ruby-throated hummingbird. The brilliant ruby throat is possessed only by the mature male. The female and young are green and white. This hummingbird is said to be capable of a flight speed of fifty-five miles per hour.

The young are fed by regurgitation. It is astonishing to watch the parent's seeming ferocity and the depth to which the needle-like bill is driven into the baby's throat.

Of the many remarkable characteristics shared by hummingbirds, probably the most striking of all is the glittering metallic or iridescent plumage of the males. Another important feature, though not so well known to most of us, is the leathery texture and strength of the skin.

Rarely found in any birds, this texture is all the more surprising in these diminutive creatures.

**The Ruby-throated Hummingbird,** *Archilochus colubris,* is a familiar bird in eastern North America. It is named for the adult male's sparkling, iridescent ruby-red throat. The upper parts are shining green, the wings and tail have a dark purplish cast, while the under parts are dull gray. In females and wintering males the lovely ruby-red color is lacking. Sometimes, after a sapsucker has bored a hole in the trunk of a maple tree, one of these birds will insert its tubular tongue in the hole to suck out the sap. Ruby-throats nest from central Canada south to Florida and as far west as North Dakota.

**Gould's Hummingbird,** *Hylonympha macrocerca,* one of the largest members of the family, was the subject of an intensive search by collectors for over seventy years. Described from a trade skin in 1873, and well represented in collections received that year by European

**AN ELUSIVE HUMMINGBIRD**

It took naturalists seventy-five years of intensive search to find the home of Gould's hummingbird, one of the most famous of these small birds. Hummingbirds are noted for their gorgeous colors, swift, perfectly controlled flight, and ability to fly backwards.

feather merchants, this hummingbird thereupon vanished into the blue. In the following years naturalists conjectured and explored extensively for this great rarity—all to no avail. It was not until 1947 that Dr. W. H. Phelps of Venezuela solved the mystery by rediscovering the bird on Cerro Azul in eastern Venezuela. Another collector had spent time halfway up this mountain without finding a trace of the hummingbird—yet in the restricted summit forest, hardly thirty miles away from busy Port-of-Spain, the bird proved abundant.

About eight inches in total length, Gould's hummingbird has a scissor-like tail that reaches a length of almost five inches. Males are glossy green, with velvet-black hind crown, upper back and tail. The forehead is sparkling violet, the under parts dull green.

**The Bee Hummingbird,** *Calypte helenae,* of Cuba and the Isle of Pines, is not only the smallest hummingbird but also the smallest feathered creature in the world. Rather rare, this tiny bird is a cousin of the much larger ruby-throat of eastern North America. Its common name aptly describes its size and general appearance in flight. The total length is something over two inches—rather large for a "bee," but more than half of this length consists of the bill and tail. The male is bright ruby on the crown, throat, and long ear tufts, with bluish-green upper parts, a still more bluish tail, and dull-gray underparts. The female looks like the male, except that the ruby coloring is replaced by green above and gray below.

**The Giant Hummingbird,** *Patagona gigas,* of the Andes, is over eight inches long and is by far the largest of the hummingbirds. This estimate is based chiefly on weight, for a few of the slender-tailed species slightly exceed it in total length. These giant hummers are reported to feed occasionally on smaller species of hummingbirds—a most unexpected example of cannibalism, and one that still arouses skepticism.

## OTHER SPECTACULAR HUMMINGBIRDS

To describe the endless variety of hummingbirds, each one more beautiful than the next, we would need a whole volume. So, we can mention only a few of them, and the salient characteristics by which they may be known. Even their common names, you will note, reflect the admiration of the naturalists who described them.

The Collared Inca, *Coeligena torquata,* of Central America, is a large blackish hummer with white chest and tail. The Guatemalan Hermit, like all members of its genus, has a greatly elongated central pair of tail feathers, tipped with white. The minute White-footed Racket-Tail, *Ocreatus underwoodi,* of Venezuela and nearby countries, is green with a needle-like bill, white thighs, and two long tail-wires tipped with tiny black flags. The Frilled Coquette, *Lophornis magnifica,* of Brazil, is perhaps the most highly adorned of small hummers with its pointed cinnamon crest, green throat, extensible white neck-fans tipped with green and black, and bronzy-green body, brownish tail, green forehead, and straight coral red bill! Anna's Hummer, *Calypte anna,* a Californian species, has a greenish bronze back, while the throat and sides of the neck are gleaming ruby red.

Another spectacular member of this numerous family is the Sappho Comet, *Sappho sparganura,* of the southern Andes, a gorgeous scissor-tailed bird fully seven inches long. Its back is deep rose, the wing and head glistening green, and the fantastic streaming tail bright bronze. The emphasis is all in the opposite direction in the case of the Sword-billed Hummer, *Ensifera ensifera,* of the high Andes, which is dark green with a perfectly incredible bill that quite overbalances the rest of the body. The tiny, rose-colored Snow-cap, *Microchera,* is a straight-billed hummer with a prominent white cap. The Heavenly Sylph, *Aglacocercus coelestis,* has tremendously elongated violet-blue scissor-like tail feathers, giving it a total length of nine inches. The Helmet-Crest, *Oxypogon guerini,* of the Andes, is amusingly decorated with a long white beard and white and black crown plumes. Gould's Sickle-bill, *Eutoxeras aquila,* a plain greenish-brown hummer of Costa Rica and Ecuador, has an amazing sickle-shaped bill. Still another bizarre species is the Streamer-tailed Hummingbird, *Trochilus polytmus,* of Jamaica. Its body is green, the head black with long ear tufts, and it sports a long pair of magnificent tail plumes (up to seven inches long), set off by a scarlet black-tipped bill.

This gives you no more than a tantalizing glimpse of the beauty and variety of hummingbirds. But "pictures speak louder than words," and if you seek closer familiarity with these feathered gems, we refer you to the striking illustrated monographs by Gould and others, which you can find in the larger libraries.

# Trogons—Beautiful, Delicate, and Shy

---

You ARE NOT likely to find many birds more attractive than the trogons with their glowing hues of carmine, orange, green, gold, and violet. The male is brilliantly attired and sometimes decorated with ornamental plumes, while the female is modestly dressed in browns and grays or only thinly washed with the brighter hues.

Unfortunately, trogons are not too robust. Their plumage is very soft, and the feathers drop easily. Their skin is remarkably delicate—so much so that ornithologists the world over are agreed that preparing a scientific specimen of a trogon calls for the most skillful kind of field taxidermy; one careless tug and the skin tears as readily as wet tissue paper. Trogons also have weak legs.

Trogons have no near relatives. An ancient tribe which epochs of geographical isolation have failed to alter appreciably, they now make their home in the tropics of Africa, Indo-Malaya, and America. There are some thirty-four known species, making up the order Trogoniformes. The discovery of a fossil trogon in France indicates that these birds formerly had a wider distribution than they have nowadays.

Trogons are rather silent birds of the deep forest or forest edge where they are usually found in pairs. They feed on insects caught on the wing, and supplement this fare with fruit. When they become vocal, they usually utter a series of gradually descending notes from high sentinel perches. They accompany these cries with jerky pulsations of the tail. Most species have a habit of sitting motionless for long periods, which makes it rather difficult to find them.

When we were in Panama we had the good fortune to observe the Massena Trogon, *Trogon massena,* in the Canal Zone. A female and her mate were building a nest by digging out a cavity in the side of a termite nest twenty feet up in a palm tree standing at the forest edge beside a lake. Woodpecker-like they clung to the nest and chopped

**1076**

with their bills, frequently pausing to rub off the termite grubs which stuck to their heads and eyes. Many trogons nest in rotting trees, using holes which they dig themselves or take over. The female lays from two to four white, pale blue, or pale green eggs. The nestlings are naked when they emerge.

**The Quetzal,** *Pharomachrus mocinno,* the national bird of Guatemala, is considered by many the most beautiful bird in the world. Once the sacred bird of the Aztecs, the quetzal was associated with the worship of their benign god Quetzalcoatl, for whom they mistook Cortez when he came through the pass which bears his name, and descended like a scourge into the valley of Mexico.

**THE QUETZAL—SACRED BIRD OF THE AZTECS**

The green, scarlet, black and white quetzal is one of the outstandingly beautiful birds of the world. Its brilliant green train, two feet long, enhances its striking appearance.

Partly because of the quetzal's beauty, partly because of its sacred status, the Aztecs used its feathers for royal adornment.

You can distinguish the quetzal from all other trogons by the enormous length of the feathers above the tail which sometimes extend a good two feet—or even more—beyond the true tail. The quetzal has a large, rounded crest. Its upper parts are a rich, glittering green, as are the under parts from the head to the chest. The abdomen is scarlet, while the tail is black with broad white areas and the saber-like long feathers of the back are iridescent green. In parts of South America, natives call this bird the mountain hummingbird, but we may take it that the name is suggested by the brilliance of its plumage rather than by the method of flight. However, it is true that trogons frequently flutter as they feed on fruit.

Striking as the quetzal's train is, there is at least one time when it is a definite nuisance. This is when the male aids his mate in incubating the eggs in a cramped hole in a tree. While sitting on the eggs, he bends the long feathers forward over his back and head.

In the mountains of southern Arizona we find a notable number of Mexican birds that reach only that area of the United States. Among them is the lovely Coppery-tailed Trogon, *Trogon ambiguus*, the northernmost member of the family in America.

# Mousebirds or Colies—They Creep About

THE CURIOUS little mousebird of Africa was named for its habit of creeping about among the twigs of trees, where it feeds on fruit. Not much larger than a sparrow, the mousebird has a long pointed tail that brings its total length to about twelve inches. It is brown or tan in color, tinted with blue, and it sports a jaunty crest. (There are several species, making up the order Coliiformes.) Not closely related to other birds, the mousebird does resemble the trogons in some ways. Its nest is a simple open cup, and the eggs are spotted.

**A BIRD THAT CREEPS**

The mousebird (or coly) of Africa got its name from its curious habit of creeping about in trees in quest of fruit and green shoots. When this interesting creature climbs, for sureness of footing it spreads out its toes in the shape of an X, and keeps the bottom of the foot close to the bark. The long tail is sometimes used as a prop.

Mousebirds live both in forests and more open country, and generally travel in flocks of from three to ten. When they roost, the members of the little band may hang by their feet and pack themselves together in a mass.

The mousebird, although it is famed as a creeper, is quite capable of flight. Indeed, it flies rapidly, but only for short distances.

# Kingfishers, Hornbills, and Their Relatives

Perching quietly on a limb above a pool—sometimes twenty feet above or even higher—the kingfisher awaits a favorable moment to dive like an arrow upon some unsuspecting minnow. Disappearing in a cloud of spray, the bird usually emerges in flight with the prey firmly held in its beak. After reaching a perch, the kingfisher quickly swallows the fish, head foremost. When it lacks the right kind of perch for watching, the kingfisher with its keen eyesight can discern schools of small fish as it flies above the water; a few minutes of hovering to pick its victim, and in it dives.

Aside from the kingfishers, this order (the Coraciiformes) includes the interestingly named todies, motmots, bee-eaters, rollers, hoopoes, and hornbills. They are tropical birds for the most part—only a few, such as the Belted Kingfisher of North America, reach northern latitudes. Bright colors are the rule for these birds. When it comes to size, there is an enormous range of difference, the todies being wren-sized while some hornbills are as large as an eagle. All these birds lay white eggs in a hole in the earth or in a tree or wall.

## KINGFISHERS—BELLICOSE MONOPOLISTS

When you look at a kingfisher, you note that its head seems too large for its body. In combination with the businesslike bill (which is very large and pointed), the conspicuous crest, akin to an Indian head-dress, reflects the pugnacious disposition of these birds. Kingfishers are very belligerent even toward others of their kind; a single pair will patrol a length of stream driving away all intruders. Their harsh rattling cry—it has been likened to a police whistle—is audible for quite a distance, announcing to all kingfishers in the neighborhood that the territory is occupied. Occasionally destructive around fish hatcheries, the kingfisher lives mostly on useless or even harmful minnows.

While we find kingfishers in many parts of the world, the vast majority of the eighty-odd species—they make up the family Alcedinidae —are dwellers in the tropics. The familiar Belted Kingfisher, *Megaceryle alcyon,* of the United States, is typical of the tribe. A medium-sized, bluish-gray and white bird, it offers one of the few instances of the female being outfitted in brighter colors than her mate. The lady kingfisher has a chestnut band across the breast; the male lacks this band.

To the ancient Greeks the kingfisher was *alcyon* or *halcyon,* names that you may recognize in the phrase "halcyon days." This term harks back to an old legend that kingfishers build a floating nest on the ocean, and that the weather remains calm during the time that the eggs are being incubated. There is more charm than truth in this story, for actually kingfishers nest in hollow trees or in holes dug by the birds themselves in earthen banks. The nesting burrow of the belted kingfisher, dug in a steep bank and sometimes at a considerable distance from water, may be four feet or more in length.

The kingfisher builds no nest. It lays as many as eight white eggs in a rounded cavity at the end of the burrow. The bones and scales of fish are cast up by these birds in the form of pellets. What with all the fish the parents consume or feed to the babies, the nest chamber gets to be a very "fishy" place indeed.

## OLD WORLD KINGFISHERS—INCLUDING A LAUGHING JACKASS

**The Australian Laughing Jackass or Kookaburra,** *Dacelo novaeguineae,* is the most unusual of the kingfishers, and the largest. This bird's cry is a discordant, abrupt laugh, said to be even more startling than the hyena's. As a rule the kookaburra does not catch fish, feeding instead on crabs, large insects, mice, rats, and reptiles. During the nesting season of small birds, the kookaburra often robs their nests. Not all the kingfishers of the Old World are "fishers" in the literal sense of the word; in fact, many of them have feeding habits similar to the kookaburra's.

The laughing jackass is rather pleasantly patterned in brown over most of its body. Some of its cousins in the Oriental region go in for more brilliant colors—maroon and metallic blues. The long-tailed Paradise Kingfishers, *Tanysiptera,* are perhaps the most beautiful of the family. It is a pity that since they inhabit the thinly settled coasts of New Guinea and nearby islands, few of us can ever have an opportunity to appreciate their beauty.

**THE LAUGHING JACKASS OF AUSTRALIA**
The laughing jackass, also known as the kookaburra, is a member of the kingfisher family. This bird has a strange laughlike cry that is more startling than mirthful. It feeds on such creatures as crabs, rats, mice, and reptiles.

## TODIES—BIRDS OF THE WEST INDIES

We find these curious little birds only in the West Indies, where each of the larger islands has its own distinct species. No larger than a wren, the birds, all members of the family Todidae, have a bright green back ·and scarlet throat. They have a habit of sitting quietly on a twig in the shade and making occasional sallies after flying in-

*Michigan Conservation Department*

**DANGEROUS FLUFF-BALL**

This half-grown great horned owl already shows the vicious disposition characteristic of its species. The young of many predators, if taken early and properly cared for, will grow into reasonably docile pets, but great horned owls usually prove intractable and are best let alone. Unlike other birds, owls retain a soft down fringe on their feathers which muffles the sound of their flight and enables them to sweep on their prey in almost complete silence.

### BROAD-TAILED HUMMINGBIRD FLYING BACKWARDS

These striking images are all of the same bird, taken from left to right by successive flashes of an electronic high-speed photographic unit. They show how the hummer, as it leaves the tube from which it has been sucking honey, flies backward and upward.

### THE BELTED KINGFISHER—A SKILLED FISHERMAN

The belted kingfisher hovers above the water until it detects a fish and then plunges head foremost after its victim. Its strong, heavy bill seizes the fish and holds it securely until it can be carried to a convenient perch and swallowed. The kingfisher is a belligerent bird, ready to challenge any others of its kind that attempt to trespass on its favorite fishing grounds.

sects, which they seize in their broad, flat bills. Like the motmots, to whom they are most nearly related, they dig holes in the earth where they lay their clutch of white eggs.

## MOTMOTS—THEY TRIM THEIR TAILS

Handsome, graceful, medium-sized birds, the motmots of tropical America have a peculiar racket-tipped tail. Male and female are dressed alike, and immature birds resemble the grownups—with the difference that adults may have incomplete rackets on the tail. We are told that motmots clip the tail shafts with their bills, thus form-

THE MOTMOT TRIMS ITS TAIL

An attractive bird, the motmot is famous for its supposed habit of trimming off its tail feathers with its bill until the tail takes on a racket shape. It twitches its tail from side to side in a curious manner—perhaps the racket-tips serve as a signal.

ing their racket shape. However, the feathers in the "notch" areas are weaker, and perhaps shear off through the normal action of preening. Whatever the answer may be, we know that the plumes are removed slowly, sometimes along one side of the feather at a time, sometimes on both sides, until nothing but the nude shaft remains to link the "flag" to the remainder of the tail.

We do not know how this habit of trimming the tail originated, nor do we know what possible useful purpose it may serve. The tail jerks nervously whenever the motmot sounds its notes (for which it is named), and it is twitched occasionally as the bird perches quietly in the lower portions of the gloomy tropical jungle. It may be that such actions serve as a bond between a pair of motmots.

There are eight species of motmots, all members of the family Momotidae and all related to the todies of the West Indies, and probably to the bee-eaters of the Old World. They are equipped with a black bill that has notched or saw-toothed edges. The largest of the clan, the Common Motmot, *Momotus momota,* of South America and Mexico, is fourteen inches long. It has yellowish-olive plumage with a spot of black on the chest, a black face, and a cobalt-blue crown and tail flags. The smallest and most primitive of these birds, the starling-sized Tody Motmot, *Hylomanes momotula,* of southern Mexico and Central America, is dull green and brown with a cinnamon head and neck, and bright-green eye stripes. This bird does not trim its tail in the manner we have described.

Motmots perch at moderate heights above the ground, often near water. They are usually thinly distributed, and we have learned to expect no more than a pair, or a solitary individual, for every mile or so of jungle trail. Motmots capture insects in flight, darting out from low perches like flycatchers. However, they are less likely to be attached to any single perch than many flycatching birds are. The motmot's nest may be an abandoned woodpecker hole or a tunnel which the birds dig near the water. The female lays three or four glossy white eggs, which are incubated by both parents.

## BEE-EATERS—HANDSOME BIRDS

Bee-eaters spend much of their time swooping gracefully through the air in search of bees and other insects. They are sociable birds, uttering mellow notes while on the wing to aid the members of a flock in keeping together. When ready to nest, the colony selects a bank and each pair digs a nesting burrow.

**The Common Bee-eater,** *Merops apiaster,* is one of the twenty-four species of bee-eaters. (They make up the family Meropidae.) Like their cousins the rollers, these birds are natives of the warmer parts of the Old World. The common bee-eater may nest as far north as

Denmark, but its true home extends from the south of Spain and France through the Mediterranean area to Persia and beyond. It is highly migratory, wintering in South Africa.

**A BIRD THAT FEEDS ON BEES**
The bee-eater is an exceptionally good-looking bird and a graceful flier. It feeds not only on bees, but on other insects as well. Though the bee-eater may nest as far north as Denmark, it prefers the warmer regions.

This bee-eater is a marvel of softly blended pastel shades. Its upper parts are largely chestnut brown becoming reddish yellow on the rump. The wing and tail quills are bluish green, the former tipped with black. A band of deep blue-black extends around the throat. With its long, pointed wings and greatly elongated central tail feathers, the bird is able to float through the air with all the ease of a swallow. Some of the African bee-eaters are even more attractive, and few birds can match them in beauty.

## ROLLERS—ANOTHER GROUP OF GRACEFUL BIRDS

At times, particularly when they are courting, these birds roll and tumble through the air—hence the name "roller." They are colorful birds. The tint of the head, neck, and breast in many rollers is that peculiar greenish blue that artists term "verditer." The back is a warm chestnut-brown changing to purple on the lower back.

This small Old World family of sixteen species (the Coraciidae) is related to the kingfishers and motmots. We find these birds mainly in the tropics, but the Common Roller, *Coracias garrulus,* nests as far north as Denmark. Rollers lay their white eggs in the cavity of a tree.

**The Oriental Roller or Dollarbird,** *Eurystomus orientalis,* gets its curious common name from a light-bluish area in its wings the size of a silver dollar. We find this bird all the way from southern Siberia to Australia. The Siberian birds migrate south into the Philippines and East Indies; those of Australia migrate north into New Guinea and nearby islands. A dark blue creature with a red bill, the dollarbird chooses a conspicuous perch on a dead limb while on the lookout for flying insects, and swoops after any it may spy. Many American soldiers stationed in the South Pacific during the war became familiar with this colorful bird.

Several of the African rollers have a long pointed tail, and are even more graceful in appearance than their Asiatic cousins. The curious Ground-rollers of Madagascar have longer legs and shorter wings than the other members of the family. As you might therefore expect, they spend much time on the ground or in low bushes.

## HOOPOES—NAMED FOR THEIR MELLOW CALL

**The Hoopoe,** *Upupa epops,* named after its mellow call, "hoo-poo," makes its home in many parts of the Old World north to France. The long crest that runs the length of its crown, makes it a conspicuous bird as it stalks along the ground nodding its head and expanding and contracting the crest. About a foot in length, the hoopoe has a variegated pattern of white, buff, and black. Its oil glands have a disagreeable odor.

The hoopoe's food is largely insects—particularly ants, which it digs from the ground with its long, curved beak. The nest is placed in a hollow tree, and once the female begins incubating she is fed by her mate and hardly ever leaves the nest. In this respect the hoopoes are like the hornbills. Hoopoes compose the family Upupidae.

In Africa we find two or three birds related to the hoopoe but more at home in trees. They are called tree-hoopoes, and sometimes placed in a separate family.

**HOOPOE—A BIRD WITH INDIAN HEADDRESS**

An Old World bird, the hoopoe has been named for its call. The hoopoe's favorite food is ants—its long, curved beak is ideally shaped for prying them out of the ground. Its conspicuous crest gives it a very amusing appearance.

## HORNBILLS AND THEIR REMARKABLE NESTING HABITS

Hornbills are medium-sized or large birds that dwell in Asia and Africa, usually in the jungles. Their most prominent feature, as you can gather from their name, is the very large bill, which bears a sizable, brightly colored, horny growth—the casque. Though the bird has the appearance of being out of balance, the casque is generally very light, being made up largely of thin-walled hollow cells.

The hornbill is famous, and deservedly so, for its unique nesting habits. Once courtship and mating are over, the female retires to a hollow tree and seals herself into the chamber with an adobe-like substance made up of dung and pellets of mud. These materials the male gathers on the forest floor and swallows. Later he expels them in the form of small saliva-permeated pellets which he "hands" to the female who remains inside the nest. She promptly plasters them on the sides of the entrance. At last only a slitlike window remains which is just big enough to receive part of the bill. For the next six or eight weeks the attentive and anxious male feeds the female through this opening. The imprisoned female lays a few white eggs. While incubating, she begins a complete molt and for a time is flightless, having lost all her wing and tail feathers.

Among many hornbills the female breaks her way out of the nest a week or more before the young are ready to leave the shelter. Dressed in a fresh cloak of feathers, she helps her mate feed the young. With an amazing display of instinct, the babies immediately rebuild the entrance barrier. At this stage they are comical little fellows that sit like tiny little penguins with the long tail clamped tightly to their backs. They assume this posture even when removed from the nest.

Most hornbills are black and white, sometimes varied with chestnut or gray. Their legs and feet are short and rather weak, except in the curious African Ground Hornbills, *Bucorvus,* which catch many insects and even mice—whereas the more typical hornbills are fruit-eaters. The two species of ground hornbills also differ from all the others in not plastering shut the entrance to the nest. Some forty-six species make up the family.

In their native habitat, hornbills are active birds of the forest canopy. Leaping from bough to bough and thrashing lightly about on the tips of the tallest fruiting trees, they usually appear not in the least encumbered by the ungainly bill. Their flight is heavy and sluggish. In the morning and evening the hornbill is likely to descend to the ground to feed, bathe, and collect damp earth. At such times, instead of walking soberly along as might be expected of such a large bird, it hops about ludicrously.

Among the members of this family (the Bucerotidae) we find several that are especially amusing in behavior or appearance. One of these is the Rufous Hornbill or Calao, *Buceros hydrocorax,* of the Philippines. Without a doubt this bird is the most obstreperous denizen of the forest, because of its powerful, oft-repeated cry and its unbelievably noisy flight—a sound which has the hissing quality of a low glider or defective bomb. A former infantryman we know insists that he was once in an open column of men moving along a forest road on Bataan when the point man, hearing the wind whistling through the wings of a low-flying hornbill, hit the dirt instinctively.

Among the largest members of the family is the Rhinoceros Hornbill, *Buceros rhinoceros*, named for the shape of its casque. The Helmeted Hornbill, *Rhinoplax vigil*, of the East Indies, has central tail feathers some three or four feet long. Its total length is as much as

**THE RHINOCEROS HORNBILL—JUNGLE GIANT**
All hornbills have a very prominent bill—the striking shape of the one belonging to the rhinoceros hornbill is responsible for its name. The members of the hornbill clan are noted for their unique nesting habits—the female seals herself in the nest with mud!

six feet. Unlike the tail feathers of other birds, the two central tail feathers do not drop out and molt together. Instead, they are replaced alternately, so that at least one of these long tail feathers is always present to act as a rudder.

# Woodpeckers, Toucans, Honey Guides, and Their Relatives

THESE BIRDS are climbers and diggers. They all have a "yoke-toed" foot with two toes directed backward and two forward. This arrangement is obviously useful to woodpeckers in climbing on tree trunks; the other birds of this order often have somewhat similar habits, though they are less specialized for climbing and for digging in wood. Woodpeckers, the best-known family, are found in most parts of the world except Australia and New Guinea. The jacamars, puffbirds, and toucans make their home in the American tropics. As for the honey guides and barbets, they also live in the tropics—the former in Africa and Asia, the latter in both the Old World and the New.

The birds belonging to this group (the order Piciformes) lay white eggs in a hole in a tree or occasionally in the earth. As a rule they dig this nesting chamber themselves. The honey guides have parasitic habits, laying their eggs in the nests of other birds—particularly their cousins, the barbets. Toucans and barbets are generally brightly colored, woodpeckers and jacamars somewhat less so, while the puffbirds and honey guides are often plain brown or gray, sometimes with a patch of yellow on the back.

## JACAMARS—QUIET BIRDS OF THE FOREST

Jacamars haunt the outer edge of high tropical forest, overlooking grassy fields and meandering streams. They sally out after flying insects from favorite perches, but when they are not actively feeding they often sit quietly and inconspicuously for long periods.

Ranging from southern Mexico to southern Brazil, the fifteen spe-

1090

cies of jacamars—they comprise the family Galbulidae—are starling-sized, with a long, slender tail and a long, almost straight bill. They are usually glossy and bronzy green above, dull cinnamon or blackish brown below, and often the throat is white. Male and female are colored alike. Their nest is a narrow burrow drilled deep into a shallow bank; sometimes a tree cavity is used. The female lays three glossy white eggs, and the young are born blind and naked. But both parents help feed the young, and if the female meets with an accident her mate will take complete care of the chicks.

Perhaps the most beautiful of the jacamars is the Great Jacamar, *Jacamerops aurea,* of central and northern South America. About twelve inches long, it has glistening, bronzy-green upper parts, a slightly curved bill, a glossy green chin, a white throat, and cinnamon-colored under parts. The Paradise Jacamar, *Urogalba dea,* has a broad white throat. It is a slender bird ten inches long with a dark brownish head and generally blackish plumage with deep green and blue reflections. The Bronzy-breasted Jacamar, *Galbula leucogaster,* is eight inches long with a bronze-green body, white throat, and bluish head.

## PUFFBIRDS—BLASÉ AND ALOOF

Fearless though rather inactive birds of the forest, puffbirds have the same blasé aloofness as jacamars, often completely ignoring man or appearing half asleep. The way puffbirds expand the fluffy plumage of the crown and neck gives us the origin of their name. They are related to the jacamars, but instead of the glossy sheen of those birds they have plain black, brown, or blue plumage. There are thirty species of puffbirds. They make up the family Bucconidae, and they all live in tropical America, from southern Mexico to Argentina. Most of them dwell on the forest edge or on savannas containing trees and bushes, usually near water; a few live in the middle and lower tiers of deep forest.

Of these forest dwellers, the Lance-billed Puffbird, *Micromonacha lanceolata,* of northern South America, is the smallest—only five inches in length. With its coffee-brown upper parts, white under parts with blackish spots and streaks, it has the appearance of a miniature wood thrush. The Black-collared Puffbird, *Bucco capensis,* is peculiar-looking because of its huge head. A starling-sized bird, it is chestnut above, strongly marked with black wavy lines. A distinctive black band encircles the body in the region of the chest and shoulders. This bird and the Swallow-wing, *Chelidoptera tenebrosa,* are perhaps the most familiar puffbirds of the open forest edge where they hunt insects like flycatchers.

Very quiet, if not mute, most puffbirds frequently sit motionless for long periods. But the nunbirds, which are members of this family, often emit whistling notes when traveling in flocks in the company of ant wrens, ant shrikes, and woodhewers in deep forest. The White-bearded Nunbird, *Monasa morphoeus,* of South America, is typical of this group. It is a blackish-gray, thrush-sized bird with a scarlet bill encircled by white feathers. Bonaparte's Puffbird, *Notharchus hyperrhynchus,* is one of the largest of the family. Ranging from southern Mexico to South America, it is a kingfisher-like bird with a heavy black bill, black body; the forehead, throat, collar, and under tail coverts are all white.

All puffbirds nest in holes either in trees or in earthen banks. Their eggs are glossy white.

## BARBETS—PRACTICALLY INVISIBLE IN THE TREETOPS

As an aid in the process of funneling insects into its mouth, the barbet has a frame of hairlike feathers on its somewhat oversized bill. It was this characteristic that suggested the word *barbu* ("bearded") to the French ornithologist Brisson, leading to the coining of the name "barbet." Like the bill, this bird's head is also somewhat large for its small or moderately sized but stocky body.

The seventy-odd species of barbets (family Capitonidae) all have short legs and are equipped with paired toes directed forward and backwards as in their near relatives, the toucans and woodpeckers. But—notably unlike the woodpeckers—the barbets are weak climbers; they prefer to hop and walk about on their thin limbs rather than ascend vertical surfaces. They are partial to dwelling in treetops, where, despite their brilliant coloring, they are invisible in silhouette.

The green and yellow Crimson-breasted Barbet of the Philippines, *Megalaima haemacephala,* is rarely seen because it is perfectly quiet while feeding and moves about with great deliberation. In the village of Lamao on southern Bataan, flocks of these barbets came regularly to a tall fruiting tree. to feed, although local boys peppered them daily with slingshots, killing quite a few. During a brief stroll we noticed one of these barbets as it clung to the side of a stub and hammered noisily with its bill at what was evidently to be a nesting burrow. All barbets dig their nesting chambers in this way—but only in rotten wood, for their bill is by no means so efficient a chisel as a woodpecker's. Some of the African barbets are sociable, several pairs nesting in the same dead tree.

Nearly all barbets have patches of bright plumage. For example, the sparrow-sized Yellow-breasted Tinkerbird, *Pogoniulus erythonotus*, of Central Africa, has a brilliant crimson rump. The starling-sized Blue-throated Barbet, *Megalaima asiatica,* of Indo-Malaya, is purplish blue on the face, neck, and upper chest, with bright patches of scarlet on the crown and chest. The Many-colored Barbet, *Capito versicolor,* of South America, is an aptly named, sparrow-sized, greenish bird. It has golden yellow on the cheeks and chest, a broad, incomplete, lavender collar, and vivid patches of scarlet on the head, throat, and lower chest. Thus you see that the bright colors of barbets are often gaudy and clashing.

## WOODPECKERS—CLIMBERS, BORERS, DRUMMERS

Woodpeckers are such familiar birds that it is easy for us to take them for granted, forgetting about the many ways that nature has equipped them for their lifework—constantly digging in wood to find grubs, or to make holes in which to sleep and nest. In almost all of the 225 or so known kinds of woodpeckers, we find a bill that is strong and chisel-shaped. They have powerful neck muscles to give the bill extra driving strength, and the bony structure of the head is modified to resist the constant hammering to which it is subjected. The woodpecker has a long tongue which it can thrust out for a remarkable distance. Little barbs on the tip help pull grubs from their burrows. Incidentally, what makes it possible for the woodpecker to protrude its tongue so far is an arrangement much like the hummingbird's—the hyoid (tongue) bones are extremely long and curve around beneath and in back of the skull; then they run forward on top of the skull beneath the skin until they reach the forehead.

But this by no means concludes the list of the woodpecker's special equipment. Its feet are powerful, its claws strong and sharply hooked; two toes point forward, two sideways and backward. The tail feathers are stiff and pointed—excellent for a prop when the bird is clinging to a tree trunk. If you have ever watched a woodpecker at work, you have noticed that it climbs trees by a series of short hops, and not by a continuous alternate movement of the legs.

Almost all woodpeckers nest in holes in trees. As a rule they construct their own housing; a few, the flicker, for example, sometimes use a birdhouse or a ready-made cavity. The eggs are a glossy, pure white—four to eight in a clutch. When hatched, the young are naked and homely. As they grow older they become very noisy when hungry, and they utter loud, hissing or rasping cries. Among several members of the woodpecker tribe (it is known as the family Picidae) the proverbial solicitude of the mother is at a low ebb; the male is more active than his mate when it comes to feeding the young, and sometimes the mother loses all interest in her offspring long before they leave the nest.

**The little Downy Woodpecker,** *Dendrocopos pubescens,* is the best known of all the American species. It is slightly larger than a sparrow, and you can distinguish it by the sharply barred black and white pattern of its plumage. Like many other woodpeckers, the male has a bright crimson spot on the back of his head.

Woodpeckers often attract our attention by a loud tapping as they dig in soft wood. So ingrained is this habit that the woodpecker's usual "song" is really a drumming produced by tapping on a resonant dead limb. The bird performs so rapidly that your eye cannot follow the movements of its head, nor can your ear separate the rolling notes. The downy woodpecker also utters a whinny-like series of high-pitched notes and a sharp "peent" of alarm.

The Hairy Woodpecker, *Dendrocopos villosus,* looks very much like the "downy" except that it is larger, about the size of a starling. Unlike its smaller cousin, which is partial to orchards or shade trees, the hairy woodpecker favors rather extensive woodlands.

**The Flicker,** *Colaptes auratus,* spends a great deal of time feeding on the ground, often hopping about like a robin. It is very fond of ants, and consumes a good many other insect pests. At times it feeds on tree trunks or branches like other woodpeckers, and the nest chamber it digs in soft wood has the general shape of a gourd or summer squash.

The flicker has a variety of loud notes—one of them sounds like "flick-er," and there we have the origin of its common name. Its scientific name *auratus* ("golden") is derived from the gold color of the under surface of the wings. Found throughout North America, it is a large and conspicuous woodpecker. Its basic color is brown, and it is barred above and spotted below with black, with a prominent white patch on the lower back. The male has black, mustache-like marks on the side of the head, and a red nape. These marks vary somewhat in different parts of the continent.

## FLYCATCHING WOODPECKERS

Though most woodpeckers live upon insects of one sort or another, they also take fruits and nuts. The California Woodpecker or Acorn Woodpecker, *Melanerpes formicivorus,* drills long rows of shallow holes in a tree trunk. In each hole it sticks an acorn, which it may eat later when food is scarce.

Another method of feeding hardly to be expected of woodpeckers is capturing flying insects in midair. The beautiful Redheaded Woodpecker, *Melanerpes erythrocephalus* ("red head"), frequently sallies out from a telephone pole or other exposed perch after large flying insects. This good-looking woodpecker has a black and white body which effectively sets off its crimson head. Common in the Midwest, it is found only locally in the eastern part of the United States.

The large and handsomely colored Lewis Woodpecker, *Asyndesmus lewis,* named after one of the famous leaders of the Lewis and Clark Expedition, dwells in the Great Basin region of the United States. This bird, which captures insects every bit as gracefully as a flycatcher, is a rich, glossy black above, and gray, tinged with salmon red, below. On a recent trip to Sonora, Mexico, we were told by the local boys that the *carpintiero negro,* as they call this bird, lived in the vicinity in winter. Soon we saw several Lewis woodpeckers hawking for insects from the top of a large dead tree.

## SAPSUCKERS

The Sapsuckers, *Spyrapicus,* have literally tapped another source of food. In springtime they dig long rows of holes in the bark of trees and later return to drink the sap oozing from these wounds. In this way they often do considerable damage to fruit trees.

In the San Francisco Mountains of Arizona we once traced a noisy clattering echoing through the forest; we were amused to find a sapsucker using a tin sign as a sounding board for its drumming.

## PILEATED AND IVORY-BILLED WOODPECKERS

The largest woodpecker of general occurrence in North America is the Pileated Woodpecker or Logcock, *Dryocopus pileatus* (from *pileum*, a crest). An imposing bird with flaming red crest and contrasting black and white plumage, it is only slightly smaller than a crow.

**A WOODPECKER THREATENED WITH EXTINCTION**

The magnificent ivory-billed woodpecker, once common in the southern United States, is almost extinct. Woodpeckers are wonderfully adapted for pecking and drumming on wood —they have a chisel-shaped bill, a modified bony structure of the head to resist hammering, and powerful feet to get a strong grip on tree trunks.

It possesses great strength and digs large furrows and holes in trees to get at its favorite food, carpenter ants. These ants attack the heart wood of trees, entering from the base; so, to reach them the logcock must often drill through two or three inches of hard wood. Like most other woodpeckers, this species does not migrate. During the winter it digs a sleeping chamber for itself in a large tree.

The magnificent Ivory-billed Woodpecker, *Campephilus principalis,* was formerly found throughout the southern United States, but it is almost extinct. Similar to the pileated woodpecker in appearance, it was larger and had a huge ivory-white bill. It was at home in primeval forests, and the widespread lumbering operations of recent years doomed it. Related ivory-bills live in Cuba and Mexico, but their numbers are greatly reduced.

## OTHER WOODPECKERS

The Wryneck, *Jynx torquilla,* is an Old World bird named for its habit of twisting its neck while peering about for food. It is a peculiar and primitive woodpecker—its tail feathers are not modified for clinging to tree trunks. Like the American flicker, but to a greater extent, it feeds on the ground upon ants or other insects.

The Piculets (diminutive of *Picus,* a woodpecker) are tiny birds, much smaller than a house sparrow. We find them in the tropics of both hemispheres. Like the wrynecks, they have unmodified tails. However, instead of feeding on the ground, they climb around on branches in search of insects, more or less in the manner of nuthatches.

## TOUCANS AND THEIR HUGE BILLS

The toucan's bill is so large that when you see it you wonder how the bird can maintain its balance. The fact is that this inflated bill, though strong, is very light. While the toucan has no trouble standing, it might well have some when it comes to bedding down. However, the bird solves this problem ingeniously by packing itself up in a systematic manner. First the head is turned backward and laid sidewise on the top of the back. Then the fanlike tail is spread out and folded over the gaudy bill and back!

Some naturalists have suggested that the toucan uses this long bill to reach otherwise inaccessible fruits or berries. But this theory seems far fetched and does not explain the brilliant color pattern of the toucan bill, which varies from species to species and very likely is of value in courtship or pairing.

The thirty-seven species of these huge-billed birds (the family Ramphastidae) live in tropical forests ranging from Mexico to Argentina. We find most of them near sea level, with a small number reaching high elevations in the Andes. Though the toucans' closest kinship is with the barbets and woodpeckers, the large bill reminds us of the hornbills of Asia and Africa. Indeed, we find many similarities in habit between toucans and hornbills. Both feed on fruit and seeds and relish young birds, eggs, and insects. Both nest in cavities high in forest trees. In flight, both are sluggish though not ungraceful, thrashing the air noisily with their pinions, with the hornbill much the louder. Another point of resemblance is that both birds are noisy screamers.

Toucans, some of whom cry "tucano"—hence the name—often gather in flocks on high branches of the forest. There they seem to be arguing violently, lifting their bills together, chattering hoarsely, their bugling synchronized with rapid upward swings of the massive bill. Because of this trait they are called "preacher birds" in some localities.

The largest of the toucans, the Toco, *Ramphastos toco,* is crow-sized. It is black, with the rump, throat, and sides of face and neck white, the under tail coverts scarlet, the eye-ring blue, and the bill orange banded with black. Related toucans have yellow or orange on the throat or rump. The Gray-breasted Toucan, *Andigena hypoglaucus,* another large bird, dwells in the northern Andes from Colombia to Peru. Deep brownish green above, it has a black crown, yellow rump, and reddish-tipped tail. The under parts are pale bluish gray. The least noticeable and little known members of the family, the Tucanets, *Aulacorhynchus,* are greenish birds with a much smaller bill. They live in mountain rain forests—sometimes at altitudes of eight thousand feet. We have found them dwelling in the crowns of great mist-cloaked trees.

The most unbelievable member of the toucan tribe is the Curl-crested Aracari, *Beauharnaisius,* of Peru and Brazil. This bird has a head covering of curled and rumpled cellophane-like crown feathers. Otherwise it is modestly dressed in dark green with red on the back,

### AUSTRALIA'S SUPERB LYREBIRD

The adjective is actually a part of this bird's name and is used to distinguish it from the only other member of the family, Albert's lyrebird, which lacks the remarkable tail plumes. Originally thought to be related to the pheasants, the rooster-size lyrebird is now recognized as belonging to the order of perching birds. The cock's outer tail feathers measure a good two feet in length, and are whitish marked with a deep brown; the central lace-like feathers are white. The female lays only one egg at a time, and both incubation and the development of the young are comparatively slow processes.

### THIS NEST IS BUILT TO LAST
Barn swallows build their nests largely of mud, plastering them on any convenient wall as long as some slight support is available—even the dubiously secure nail-and-horseshoe arrangement on a barn—and may use the same nest year after year. Feathers, usually obtained from a nearby chicken yard, make this sturdy structure very comfortable for the four or five little barn swallows. Often there are two broods a year.

rump, and flanks. Another interesting toucan is the Collared Aracari, *Pteroglossus torquatus*, of Mexico and northern South America. A medium-sized bird with a scarlet rump, reddish collar, and a red and yellow breast, it has bill markings that resemble huge saw teeth.

We are told that toucans are easily tamed and make amusing pets.

**THE TOCO—BIGGEST OF THE TOUCANS**

The toucan's brightly colored bill is so large that the bird has to make elaborate sleeping arrangements. First it turns its head backward and lays it sidewise on the top of its back. Then it spreads out its tail like a fan, folding it over the bill and back. Now the toucan is ready for sleep! Toucans are noisy—they are sometimes called "preacher birds."

## HONEY GUIDES—THEY HAVE A PASSION FOR HONEYCOMB

The scientific name of the Common Honey Guide, *Indicator indicator*, tells you that this bird points out something. The story behind that name is one of the most fascinating you may encounter among any birds. What this honey guide does is to indicate or point out the nests of wild bees to man. This it does by constantly chattering until it draws the traveler's attention, and then flying ahead until it reveals the hive! The African natives who profit by this behavior then usually break open the bees' nest and take the honey. However, they leave some of the comb for the bird, which consumes it avidly.

From what we know of birds' intelligence—or rather lack of it—we cannot believe that the honey guide reasons out this method of securing food. Rather we must suppose that over a long period of time an instinctive type of behavior has developed, with some four-footed honey-eater, perhaps the honey badger, and not man, serving as the original partner. We also have reports that the honey guide sometimes leads men to the neighborhood of leopards or venomous serpents, but these tales do not seem to have any basis in fact. Although most, if not all, honey guides are partial to honeycomb, only one or two species have evolved this "guiding" behavior.

Another remarkable trait of honey guides is that they are all parasitic in their nesting habits. They usually impose their eggs on hole-nesting birds, especially the related barbets. The young honey guide is then hatched and reared by the foster parent. At the time of hatching the little honey guide has a wicked-looking hook at the end of its bill. Perhaps it uses this hook to kill the young barbets or other baby birds in whose home it finds itself. After the honey guide is a few days old this hook disappears.

This family (the Indicatoridae) contains only eleven species, all somberly colored birds of little or no economic importance. Two species dwell in Asia, the rest in Africa.

**The African Lyre-tailed Honey Guide,** *Melichneutes,* though found over most of the African forests, is still very rare in museum collections. The central tail feathers of this bird are somewhat lengthened and lyrate (shaped like a lyre), while the outer ones are short and stiff. Dr. James P. Chapin, one of the few naturalists who have seen and collected the lyre-tailed honey guide, believes that these specialized tail feathers are the source of a mysterious, intermittent, nasal or whining sound often heard high above the forest. The bird swoops through the air and its tail feathers vibrate, producing the sound. Even the keen-eyed natives are uncertain as to the origin of this sound, although some of them admit it is produced by a bird. The small size and dull coloring of this honey guide make it difficult to trace the noise to its source. It is hard to see any small moving object through the high canopy of jungle trees against the brilliant sky.

**The Himalayan Honey Guide,** *Indicator xanthonotus,* is likewise something of a bird of mystery, as it had not been seen in over fifty years up to recent times. But a few years ago Dr. Walter Koelz observed considerable numbers of them visiting wild bees' nests along rocky ridges in Nepal. Another naturalist—this time in Burma—saw one of these honey guides catching insects like a flycatcher. The Himalayan honey guide's tail feathers are somewhat stiffened and short-

**IT "PLAYS ITS LYRE" ABOVE THE JUNGLE**
The lyre-tailed honey guide is the most mysterious member of the fascinating honey-guide group. As it zooms high above the jungle, the air rushes through its stiff, lyre-shaped tail feathers, producing a whining noise. Perhaps this sound guides some forest animal to hidden honey, just the way the noise made by some other honey guides serves to reveal such a cache to man.

ened—an indication to us that it is in the early stage of the specialization we find in the African lyre-tail. The Himalayan bird has a bright yellow patch of feathers on the lower back; the other Asiatic honey guide, found in the Malay Peninsula, has duller coloring.

# Perching Birds—Greatest Group of All

MORE THAN half of the 8,600 or so species of birds belong to the huge order of perching birds. There are approximately 5,100 species in this large group. As a rule these birds are small; taken as a whole, they are without doubt the most advanced and successful of all the birds.

The order Passeriformes, as the perching birds are known, contains three main subgroups. In the first, naturalists place only the Australian Lyre-bird, and possibly one or two other peculiar Australian birds.

Then we have the true singing birds (Oscines), and those that have a less elaborate structure of the muscles of the syrinx or voice box. These last, the Clamatores (the noisemakers), seem, by and large, to be a declining group. The Old World representatives—the pittas, philepittas, broadbills, and New Zealand "wrens," are apparently getting along best on islands such as Madagascar, New Zealand, and the East Indies. The headquarters of the Clamatores is South America, but that continent was isolated for many millions of years from the other continents and has rather primitive animal forms. On the other hand, we find that some of the Clamatores—notably the Tyrant Flycatchers—have invaded North America in considerable numbers.

The Oscines or true songbirds number about four thousand species. Well represented in almost all parts of the globe, they seem to be at their most varied in the Old World tropics.

## BROADBILLS—AMONG THE HANDSOMEST OF ALL BIRDS

These birds have an unusually broad bill which they use to catch insects on the wing. Though you would gather from this method of

1102

feeding that they are active creatures, the reverse is true—they are rather sluggish. However, most broadbills are very beautiful, with reds, blues, and greens predominating in their plumage. These primitive perching birds (family Eurylaimidae) build large, hanging nests with a side entrance. They are best represented in the East Indies, though a few range as far as the Himalayas, and two are found in Africa.

The Green Broadbill, *Calyptomoena viridis*, is bright green with black spots on the sides of the head. The forehead feathers are very dense and extend forward over the bill. Two related species, found only in the mountains of Borneo, are among the prettiest of all birds. One of them has green plumage streaked with black; the other is green above, blue below.

**A SLUGGISH BUT BEAUTIFUL BIRD**
The magnificent black and red broadbill dwells in the jungles of Indo-China and the great islands of the East Indies. Its capacious bill makes short work of large insects and wild fruit. Like other broadbills, this bird is at most times a rather sluggish creature.

On the other hand, the Common African Broadbill, *Smithornis*, is a plain-colored bird. It has a curious courtship performance, in the course of which the male makes a short circular flight above its perch and produces a whirring note with its wing quills. The other African Broadbill, *Pseudocalyptomoena*, is a bright-colored little bird

found only in the mountain forests of central Africa. At one time
naturalists considered both African broadbills members of the Old
World flycatcher family. A careful study of the birds proved they
were true broadbills.

## PITTAS AND THEIR GORGEOUS COLORS

Pittas, also known as jewel thrushes, are among the most beautiful
of all the birds. They live on the ground in deep tropical and subtropical forest. We find them at their most diverse and abundant in
the Malay countries and the East Indies, but they range as far as
Africa, northern Australia, and the Philippines. They hop about on
the forest floor, feeding on insects, worms, and snails. When startled,
these lovely birds sometimes flutter along on the ground with a feeble, thrashing flight—though ordinarily they make their exit by hopping through the underbrush. The scattered and hidden individuals
maintain contact by means of loud, rather plaintive whistles, heard
chiefly in the morning and evening. They roost well above the
ground, and also sing and whistle from such elevated perches.

**THE GREEN-BREASTED PITTA**
Noted for its lovely colors, this bird of the deep tropical forest is a poor flier. It maintains contact with its fellows by means of rather plaintive whistles. Its globelike nest,
placed in thick undergrowth, has a side entrance.

The twenty-three known species of pittas (family Pittidae) are remarkably alike in structure and habits. All are plump, long-legged birds with comparatively large heads, short, rounded wings, and exceedingly short tails. The New World ant pittas—no relations—are very similar to them in form but not in color.

The more colorful pittas include Steere's Pitta, *Pitta steerei*, a bird of the Philippines with a black head, white throat, olive-green back, and sky-blue wing and abdomen—the latter with a velvety black center. Another striking member of the family is the Superb Pitta, *Pitta superba*, of the Admiralty Islands; it is velvety black with sky-blue wings and a scarlet abdomen. Perhaps the most beautiful of these birds is the Blue-tailed Pitta, *Pitta guajana*, which we find in Malaya, Sumatra, and Borneo. Its vivid colors include a rich brown above with a golden-yellow eye-stripe and hind neck, black mask and central crown, buff throat, purple tail, black and white wings, blackish-purple under parts, and brilliant orange-red chest barring.

Pittas build their nest of twigs, moss, bark, and leaves glued together with mud; the whole forming a globelike structure with an entrance in the side. It is placed on or near the ground in thick undergrowth. The female lays three to six whitish eggs peppered with purple, brown, and red.

## PHILEPITTAS—PRIMITIVE BIRDS

You have noticed in a number of earlier cases that birds dwelling on large islands are likely to include some primitive types. This observation applies to the philepitta, found only on Madagascar. It is a quiet bird of the forest undergrowth, where it lives on fruit. The Common Philepitta has smooth black plumage, and the male sports large wattles on the head. The philepittas make up the family Philepittidae.

Two other Madagascar birds (belonging to the genus *Neodrepanis*) used to be placed in the sunbird family. These birds are highly modified for sucking nectar from flowers; they have a curved bill for the purpose, and that was why naturalists included them among the sunbirds. Recent study has shown, however, that the birds are really philepittas.

## MANAKINS AND THEIR COURTSHIP DANCES

We once watched the Redheaded Manakin, *Pipra mentalis,* dance on a specially coveted limb thirty feet above the ground in a forest tree in Panama. The hard-working little fellow remained on and about his *lek* (courtship area) day after day, snapping his wings like an infuriated crapshooter at the modestly dressed females and doubtless luring some of them to tryst with him on his prepared courting stage. Thereafter the female manakins were left strictly to their own devices. Theirs was the responsibility of building the nest, incubating the eggs, and bringing up the young.

These manakins, dwellers in the American jungles, are sparrow-sized birds. The males of many of the fifty-nine species—the whole group makes up the family Pipridae—are brilliantly adorned in crimson, blue, and gold. Others, however, are dressed in the most inconspicuous of forest colors—dull olive or gray. And, as you would expect, these dull hues apply to the female manakins in general.

The typical manakin is a stocky bird with a short bill, weak legs, square tail, and curiously compressed wing bones; while the oddly formed quill feathers arising from the forearm have thick shafts. The shape of the wing bones and feathers is a key to the noise-making of the voiceless manakins—the explosive rattling and snapping of the wings. These sounds, produced during the breeding season, take the place of song in attracting a mate or warning off other males.

Gould's Manakin, *Manacus vitellinus,* of Central America, a four-inch bird, performs a very specialized courtship dance complete with elaborate wing-snapping. This bird's *lek* is on the ground. Here the male clears a doormat-sized space of every leaf and twig and guards it jealously. Dressed mainly in green, he has a vivid black crown, and black wings and tail; his throat and the sides of the face are bright orange gold.

Many other manakins are quite striking in appearance, perhaps the most spectacular being the Cirrhate Manakin, *Teleonoma fili-cauda,* a finch-sized bird with long hairy shafts sticking out one and a half inches beyond the tail. Black above with a scarlet crest, it has a canary-yellow face and under parts. The Lance-tailed Manakin, *Chiroxiphia lanceolata,* is another finch-sized black bird; its legs and crown are scarlet, the back blue. The male Helmeted Manakin, *An-*

*tilophia galeata,* is sparrow-sized, brownish black with a glistening red helmet. The female is dull olive gray. One of the most unusual species of this brilliantly colored tropical group is the puffy-throated White-naped Manakin, *Manacus candaei,* of Central America. It is black above, yellow below, with a broad white collar and long white extensible throat plumes.

## COTINGAS—EXOTIC BIRDS

This group of fascinating American tropical birds has three particularly famous members. Each of them is famous for a different feature —one for its appearance, one for its voice, and one for its courtship habits. Most of the ninety species of cotingas have attractively colorful plumage. Ranging from wren to crow size, they are frequently dressed with peculiar and bright accessory plumes, and marked with patches of blazing color. The queer-looking Umbrella Bird, *Cephalopterus ornatus,* does not fit into this picture at all. This name is a puzzling one, but, as you will see, it is appropriate. The umbrella bird is a crow-sized, bluish-black species with a tremendous extensible crest. When this crest is opened, it covers the crown and bill completely, taking on the appearance of a shaggy parasol. One species has a nude reddish chest, with a long, tassel-like wattle dangling from it.

The Bellbird, *Procnias alba,* of northern South America, is another famous member of the group. Again the name may puzzle you, and again it is apropos. This bird has an amazing bell-like voice that makes it the most conspicuous forest bird in South America. A rope-like black wattle on the forehead is lashed about the bill as this remarkable bird delivers its penetrating call from a high perch over dense forest. High on Mt. Auyantepui in southern Venezuela we once heard a marvelous bellbird chorus ringing out about a thousand feet below us and perhaps a mile away.

Another feature that helps make the bellbird the most noticeable bird of the forest is its spotless white plumage. The Ghost Cotinga, *Carpodectes nitidus,* a bird we found in Central as well as South America, has the same kind of plumage. In both cases, the females are smaller and protectively colored with green.

The other outstandingly remarkable cotinga is the Cock-of-the-Rock, *Rupicola,* a parrot-sized golden bird with black wings and an amazing disklike crest. Cotingas are related to the manakins, and have similar courtship ceremonies. The larger size of the males, and their bright coloring and fancy accessory plumes, are all indications that the female undertakes much or all of the nest-building, incubation, and care of the young. It is probable that many species of cotingas are polygamous.

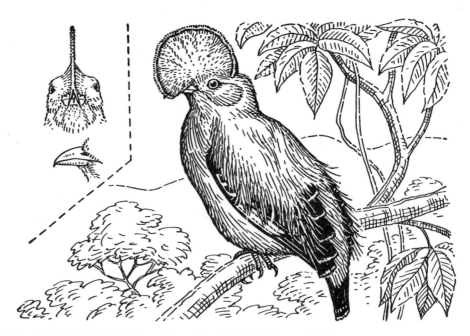

**THE COCK-OF-THE-ROCK AND ITS COURTSHIP DANCES**
One of the most bizarrely plumed of South American birds, the cock of the rock is also noted for its courtship dances. At courting time, about twenty males and females gather on and near the ground to perform noisy mating displays in special forest arenas. The inset shows (*top*) how the permanently erected crest covers the bill and (*bottom*) what the bill looks like without the crest.

In a family noted for its elaborate courtship dances, that of the cock-of-the-rock is the most famous of all. Explorer Robert Schomburgk tells of observing about twenty of these birds of both sexes perched on bushes surrounding an open space on the ground, all of them uttering cries. One male with wings and tail outspread was on stage. He walked in circles, scratching the ground, moving his wings up and down. Finally he jumped to the sidelines, apparently exhausted, as another male took his place in the ring. Schomburgk reports that the females kept calling all the while, but remained on their perches. Some cotingas carry on their courtship on the ground, others high among the branches.

Nesting methods vary also. Some species—the umbrella bird for one—build nests of sticks in tall trees; others construct hanging nests, a few make use of tree cavities, and at least one bird, the cock-of-the-rock, nests in caves. In southern Venezuela, in 1937, we found a nest of this bird on a ledge five feet above the ground in a large, dimly lit cave. It was built of mud and twigs and finely lined with black rootlets. On the floor, below the nest, were many olive-sized nuts which the birds had stripped of their fleshy husks. The eggs of this species are buff with reddish-brown and violet spots; the umbrella bird's are pure white.

Cotingas—they make up the family Cotingidae—dwell in the upper levels of the forest where they can find fruit, berries, and insects. These birds usually have harsh voices—the bellbird is an exception— and some of them, like the Capucine Monkbird, *Perissocephalus tricolor,* have a garrulous, explosive grunt reminding us of a howling monkey's. Incidentally, this aptly named pigeon-sized, cinnamon-brown cotinga has a nude bluish-gray head surrounded by a collar of bulging feathers, giving it the look of a rotund old monk with his head pulled in. Large cotingas of peculiar form are the Crimson-fruit Crows, *Haematoderus militaris,* of northern South America, which are strawberry red throughout. Another group of strange-looking birds are the Wattled Bellbirds, *Procnias tricarunculata,* of Central America; reddish with a white head and throat, they have three black, whiplike wattles springing from the base and sides of the bill.

As for the small cotingas, six to ten inches long, naturalists call them the true cotingas. Many are brightly colored, though some are grayish and nondescript with no distinction in color between male and female. A notable example of the colorful birds is the Pompadour Chatterer, one of the most exotic of the cotingas. This name was gallantly bestowed on it by an English ornithologist named Edwards, who named the gorgeous creature in honor of a famous French siren of his day, the celebrated Madame de Pompadour. One of these birds was being shipped to her when it fell prize to a British frigate.

The male Pompadour chatterer is a glistening raspberry red with hairlike feathers, twisted wing coverts, and spotless white wings. Females and immature males are gray below and slate above. An inhabitant of the forest crown, it ranges over much of South America. We found it to be rare in southern Venezuela.

The Common Gray Cotinga, *Lipaugus vociferans,* is doubtless the commonest and the most inquisitive of tropical forest birds. Robin-sized and gray, it follows the hunter tirelessly, and seems always to dart into sight whenever a disturbance occurs. The only cotinga to reach the United States is the Rose-throated Becard, *Platypsaris aglaiae,* which we find occasionally in southern Texas and Arizona. It builds a large, untidy, baglike nest.

## TYRANT FLYCATCHERS

Tyrant flycatchers are literally tyrants in their relations with other birds. Aggressive and pugnacious, they do not confine their attacks to birds their own size, but readily tackle hawks, crows, and other large birds. As for the "flycatcher" part of the name, it tells you how these birds get their living—they feed on flies and other insects. Selecting a prominent perch, the flycatcher sallies forth in pursuit of a hapless insect, seizing its victim with an audible snap of the broad, flat bill.

An interesting point about these tyrant flycatchers is that of the many families of primitive perching birds that abound in South America, the flycatchers are the only ones that have ranged northward and become an important part of the birdlife of temperate North America. Even so, the great majority of the 365 species of this large family (Tyrannidae) are native to tropical America.

### KINGBIRDS—NO RESPECTERS OF HAWKS

Woe betide any crow or hawk that approaches the kingbird's nest. Uttering a high-pitched battle cry, the kingbird sets out in hot pursuit, swooping down again and again to strike its larger but clumsier adversary on the back and shoulders. Finally it returns triumphantly home with short, quivering wingbeats. Even humans who venture to climb to its nest are given the same unceremonious reception, and have been known to fall from a tree when taken aback by the fury of this starling-sized bird's onslaught.

The Eastern Kingbird, *Tyrannus tyrannus,* is common in eastern North America during the summer; in the winter, like other northern members of the family, it migrates to tropical climes where it can find insects on the wing. Grayish black above and white below, the kingbird has a white-tipped tail, and on its crown there is a concealed red patch.

## THE PHOEBE AND ITS RELATIVES

Of far gentler demeanor than its cousin the kingbird is the familiar Phoebe, *Sayornis phoebe*. Its name comes from the throaty note it utters incessantly during the nesting season. A somberly colored bird of sparrow size, it has a brownish-black back and a black head; the under parts are grayish white.

This flycatcher likes to nest near water, attaching its feather-lined nest of mud to a niche in a rock wall or steep river bank. Now that it has learned to use man-made structures, you may sometimes find its nest on a beam below a bridge or on the rafter of an outbuilding. It lays four or five white or lightly spotted eggs.

The Wood Pewee, *Contopus virens*, is similar to the phoebe but it lives in woodlands and has a much mellower song, "Pee-a-wee" according to some, "Dear me, dear me" according to other listeners. The wood pewee is a notable nest builder, its nest being a dainty cup placed on a lichen-covered branch. The bird covers the outside of this structure with lichens attached by spider webs. The finished nest takes on the appearance of a knot or protuberance on the branch.

As for some of the other North American flycatchers—the Alder and Acadian Flycatcher, for example—many find it difficult to tell them apart, or even to distinguish them from the pewee and the phoebe. However, once you become familiar with their songs and habits, you find that each of these birds is quite distinctive.

## CRESTED FLYCATCHERS—THEY USE CAST-OFF SNAKESKINS

The Crested Flycatcher, *Myiarchus crinitus,* is noted for its habit of usually including a castoff snakeskin in its nest. We do not know what purpose, if any, this curious trait serves; but some naturalists believe that the snakeskins scare away enemies that intend to rob the nest. Nesting in holes in trees, the crested flycatcher lays eggs marked with irregular black lines. It is in eastern North America that we find this bird, which has relatives in the southwestern United States and in tropical America as well. A grayish-brown bird with chestnut on the wing and tail quills, it utters loud mellow notes that immediately attract our attention.

### ATTRACTIVE SOUTHWESTERN FLYCATCHERS

Most flycatchers have dull colors, but the Scissor-tailed Flycatcher, *Muscivora forficata*, which we find in Oklahoma and Texas and nearby areas, is one of the exceptions. It is gray, white, and buff, washed with delicate pink on the breast. The deeply forked tail is a good ten inches long. The scissortail is an interesting bird to watch. You may see it select a perch on a fence post beside some well-traveled road, opening and closing its streaming tail feathers like a pair of scissors, or dashing off in graceful pursuit of insects.

**A TYRANT FLYCATCHER**

The scissor-tailed flycatcher, like all the tyrant flycatchers, is an expert at catching flies and other insects. They are called "tyrants" because of their pugnacious nature. These birds make a practice of attacking other birds—some much larger than themselves. In flight, the tail feathers of this flycatcher open and close like a pair of scissors.

The gorgeous Vermilion Flycatcher, *Pyrocephalus* ("fire-head"), dwells in only one section of the United States—along the Mexican border in the Southwest. The male's entire head and under parts are vermilion, immediately catching your eye amidst the desert vegetation. Its fluttering, butterfly-like courtship flight is a thing of beauty.

## TROPICAL FLYCATCHERS—INCLUDING A FREEBOOTER OF THE SKY

As we have seen, northern flycatchers vary quite a bit in their nesting habits. The southern ones have exploited still other possibilities. A Panamanian flycatcher, *Legatus*, is fond of nesting in the long swinging nests of the large tropical orioles or oropendolas. Instead of merely contenting itself with an old nest, this flycatcher, with the belligerence we have observed in the family Tyrannidae, constantly badgers and chases the much larger oropendolas until they abandon their nests to their tormentor. Thus the nest becomes the flycatcher's booty.

## SHARP-BILLS—MYSTERIOUS BIRDS OF THE TROPICAL FOREST

**The Sharp-bill,** *Oxyruncus cristatus,* is the only species in this South American family. Though closely related to the flycatchers, sharp-bills differ by having a straight, sharp bill which is not hooked and fringed with hairlike plumes. They live in the upper tier of thick tropical forest, and we know little of their habits aside from the fact that they are sometimes found in the company of small tanagers. Sharp-bills—the family name is Oxyruncidae—are yellowish green above with a glossy red (usually concealed) crest. The under parts are gray to yellow with much bold black spotting.

## ANT BIRDS—HOW THEY RELY ON THE ARMY ANTS

In our quest for birds for scientific purposes in the forests of tropical South America, we learned to seek out roving columns of army ants by the peculiar noises they create. Each such column is usually made up of hundreds of thousands of running ants which flow in a blackish carpet over the forest floor, scanning every burrow, every leaf, and ascending every twig, bush, and tree.

To stand in the path of an approaching army, even when the advance patrols are still far off, is an experience that you are not likely to forget soon. You can see every kind of insect and spider fleeing for its life. Millipedes come to the surface, spiders slide stiffly down their silken shrouds to the ground. Countless kinds of insects patter on the dry leaves like rain, once they have made a panicky leap from a high perch. These creatures flee well in advance of the marauding ants that force all laggards to walk the plank to their death amidst the swirling mob below.

It is through this maelstrom of death that the ant wrens and ant shrikes weave their sprightly way. Calling shrilly, twittering and darting merrily about, they gorge themselves on the hapless insects, keeping always just ahead of the carpet of ants.

Next to hummingbirds, these ant birds are perhaps the most characteristic and abundant forest birds of the American tropics. Naturalists know of no less than 238 species of these birds; the family name is Formicariidae. Among ant birds, there is often a distinct difference in the appearance of the sexes—the male black and white, the female brown or gray. Quite a few have a concealed whitish spot on the back. Ant birds generally build crude hanging nests in low positions in deep forest. They construct their nests of fibers, roots, a few leaves, moss, and grass. The female lays two or three white, blue, or brownish eggs, usually boldly blotched or scrawled with bright brown or gray.

## ANT SHRIKES, ANT WRENS, ANT THRUSHES

Naturalists recognize three main groups of ant birds: ant shrikes, ant wrens, and ant thrushes (ant pittas). Ant wrens, the most abundant members of the family, live on or near the ground in deep jungle. They have a rather slender, moderately hooked bill, and a warbler-like tail. Traveling in groups, they are easily observed. They spend much of their time in the company of ant shrikes and wood hewers. These mixed parties, often totaling twenty birds of four or five species, are very noisy and their twittering notes can be heard for perhaps forty yards in deep forest. Such a chorus is in reality a battle cry, signifying that a column of army ants is on the move—with what consequences we have already seen.

Ant wrens vary a good deal in size and coloring, but all are rather slender birds. The tiny Amazonian Ant Wren, *Microrhopias quixensis,* a warbler-sized bird, is black with white spots on the wings, tail, and bases of the back feathers. The female is dull brown. The Pied Ant Wren, *Melanopareia maximiliani,* a long, typically slender bird about the size of a large warbler or wagtail, has a bright reddish breast with a vivid white throat, a black mask, and grayish upper parts.

The ant shrikes, which have a compressed and strongly hooked bill, live in the lower and middle tier of the tropical forest or forest edge. In the larger ant shrikes the bill is usually deeply notched. The White-barred Ant Shrike, *Thamnophilus doliatus,* a bird we find in Mexico and northern South America, is amusingly dressed like a convict in vivid black and white bars. This stocky starling-sized bird has a relatively long tail and a white crown, while the female is reddish brown though similar in form. The White-winged Fire-eye, *Pyriglena,* a bird of the Andes from Colombia to Bolivia, is velvety black with concealed white on the wing, and wine-red eyes. The most com-

THE SPOTTED ANT PITTA
The ant bird has one of the most interesting feeding techniques known in the bird world. When a column of army ants is on the move in the South American jungle, every conceivable kind of insect and spider flees from the approaching horde. At such times the ant bird makes its appearance and gorges itself on the panic-stricken insects.

ical of ant shrikes is the White-faced Ant Bird, *Pithys albifrons,* of South America. A sparrow-sized bird with a reddish-brown body and grayish wings, it has a goatlike beard and a great shaggy forehead crest, both of which are pure white. It travels in large, compact flocks near the jungle floor.

We come now to the last of the three main groups of ant birds—

the ant thrushes, or ant pittas, as they are sometimes called. Thick-billed birds living on the floor of deeply shaded forest, they often resemble large brownish thrushes with greatly elongated legs and very short tails. They are secretive creatures, among the shyest and most retiring of all birds. Yet, like the rails, they utter loud, repetitious calls. Usually found alone or in pairs, ant thrushes have a call consisting of an oft repeated hollow whistle delivered most frequently at dawn and dusk. This whistle has an exasperatingly ventriloquial quality—nature's device to aid the bird in hiding from its enemies.

We have spent numberless hours hunting the deep forests for these rare birds, and on several occasions have glimpsed some that are apparently still unknown to science. One of these, on the plateau of Mt. Macarena, in southeastern Colombia, seemed to be whistling at our very feet, yet we failed to catch more than a fleeting view of it. It is not too difficult to give a fair imitation of the whistling note, and in this way it is sometimes possible to draw the bird from its deep retreat. Under ideal circumstances it will suddenly appear out of nowhere on the top of a rock or log, perch there stiffly for a few moments—and then vanish for the day.

A typical member of this secretive ant thrush or ant pitta group is the Undulated Ant Pitta, *Grallaria squamigera,* a bird native to the northern half of South America. It has legs two and one-half inches long (more than twice the length of its stubby tail), a plump olive body, bluish-gray crown, and pale cinnamon under parts barred with black. Like its relative *Grallaria excelsa,* of the Venezuelan and Colombian Andes, this species dwells on the floor of thick, subtropical mountain forest, often at altitudes of as much as eight thousand feet.

## OVENBIRDS—FEATHERED MASONS

These inconspicuous birds of the American tropics are remarkable for one trait—their flair for nest-building which gives them their curious name. As masons they have few equals among the birds. Their ovenlike nests are built of a variety of materials—mud, twigs, sticks, leaves, and grass. Usually these elaborate structures contain an inner chamber reached by a circular passageway from a side entrance.

Some kinds of ovenbirds commonly nest about houses, placing their mud nests (which weigh five to ten pounds!) on posts, beams of sheds, and on low, flat limbs. One of these birds, the Pale-legged

Ovenbird, is somewhat smaller than a starling, with a pale ochraceous back, wings, tail, and chest, a dark-brown head with broad white eye-stripes, and whitish under parts.

These birds are desirable, cheery neighbors to have about the garden. Whenever ovenbirds place a nest within view of a house, they put the side entrance toward the house; thus, their entertaining comings and goings are easily observed. To complete one of these elaborate constructions often costs the birds several months of intermittent work. The nest, formed of vegetable fibers and mud, becomes hard and adobe-like on drying. The female lays three or four white, cone-shaped eggs in the inner chamber, which is usually lined with grass. The male assists in incubating. The birds build a new nest each year —sometimes on top of the old structures.

Ovenbirds (they make up the family Furnariidae) are generally reddish or cinnamon, and have a soft and usually square tail. They are catholic in their choice of surroundings for their living quarters. Some, as we have seen, place their nests quite close to houses. You may find others in open orchards near human habitations. Some ovenbirds dwell on the floor and middle tiers of deep forest, some on the banks of tropical and mountain streams. Some are grass dwellers, some reach the temperate zone on high mountains.

In northern South America the species most frequently encountered is the shy *Synallaxis,* a warbler-sized reddish-brown bird with soft plumage and a long soft tail. It is usually found in quiet pairs in the lower portions of thick second-growth forest. Building a bulky nest of twigs, leaves, feathers, and grass in low trees or bushes, it deposits three or four whitish or pale-blue eggs. Although it is built of light materials, the nest has the characteristic ovenlike construction.

The Sharp-tailed Creeper, *Lochmias nematura,* which dwells in the mountains of South America, is a bird of wrenlike habits. We found it living in rocky gorges on the plateau of Mt. Auyantepui in southern Venezuela, at seven thousand feet above sea level. Whenever we encountered this bird, it was always very close to swift-flowing water. Somewhat smaller than a sparrow, this creeper is chocolate brown with long, slender legs. Its under parts are distinctively whitish with vivid brownish-black scalloping. Unlike the general run of ovenbirds, the sharp-tailed creeper has a stiff tail, very much like a wood hewer's. For this reason some naturalists prefer to unite the two families.

The most untypical of the ovenbirds is probably the Colombian

"Xenops," *Xenops minutus*. Resembling a tiny wood hewer or creeper, it has reddish-brown plumage above, and grayish brown below. The feathers of the head and throat have white oval centers.

## WOOD HEWERS—CREEPER-LIKE BIRDS

These birds have a deceptive name. You might gather from it that they chop into wood in the manner of woodpeckers. This is not so; wood hewers use their bill to pick insects from crevices and holes in bark. Wood hewers spend much of their active time creeping about in trees, and are adapted for this in a number of ways.

These brown, creeper-like birds dwell in the tropical forests from Mexico to Argentina. Most of them are five to eight inches long. Of the sixty-three known species—they comprise the family Dendrocolaptidae—a few are wren-sized, while a small number attain the size of a dove. The wood hewer's tail is long and stiff with spiny tips. These serve to prop or brace the bird as it creeps about, head up, on vertical tree trunks in quest of food.

The bill is generally long, slender, and gently curved, but in several species it is sickle shaped, or small and chisel-like. The wood hewer with the most spectacular bill is the Sicklebill, *Campylorhamphus trochilirostris*. It uses its long, slender bill like a pair of forceps to pick insects from deep crevices in bark or in the axils of long leaves. As you would expect in a tree-climbing bird, the wood hewer has long toes and sharp claws.

Wood hewers, as we have seen, feed on insects and take their eggs from crevices in bark and termite nests. They hunt creeper-like on tree trunks, hopping upward from the base, usually in a spiral path, then fluttering downward to the base of a neighboring tree. Smaller species may hunt only in high limbs or on high portions of the trunk. Wood hewers nest in cavities in forest trees sometimes less than a foot from the ground. Two pure-white eggs are laid. Some wood hewers sing beautifully.

Almost all wood hewers are reddish brown or tan above, brighter on the tail, and more buffy on the under parts. Often they travel and hunt with ant birds, one or more almost always being present when a congregation of birds assembles to attack insects fleeing a column of army ants. At such times there is much twittering and excitement as the wood hewers and other birds flutter about in the lowest tier of the forest.

Although most wood hewers live entirely in trees, one species, the Patagonian Earth-creeper, *Upucerthia dumetaria*, spends a good deal of time on the ground. A pale-brown bird, it has a long, curved bill, a long, soft tail, a whitish face, and buffy under parts.

**THE WOOD HEWER DIGS OUT INSECTS**

The wood hewer creeps about on trees in search of insects. It has a bill adapted for picking insects and their eggs out of crevices in bark. Like the woodpecker, the wood hewer has strong toes suited for gripping tree trunks, and a stiffened tail which it uses as a prop. Wood hewers make their nests in tree cavities.

## TAPACULOS—SHY BUT VOCIFEROUS

The name "tapaculo" is Chilean. A word of Spanish origin, it alludes to the seeming immodesty of these cocky little birds as they strut about with tail erect and hind parts exposed.

Tapaculos are inconspicuous little birds that fly rarely, preferring to scurry rodent-fashion on the shadowy forest floor. Some species dwell on grasslands, but the great majority are at home in wooded areas. We find the twenty-eight kinds of tapaculos between Costa Rica and Patagonia—some of them to elevations of ten thousand feet in the Andes. They comprise the family Rhinocryptidae. All are very shy and, but for their habit of scolding and following intruders, it would be extremely difficult to observe them.

Most tapaculos are dark slate or brown above, gray or buff below, with straight bills and scalloped plumage. They usually place their nest, constructed of sticks, grass, and moss, near the ground in a bush.

The Rufous-vented Babbler or Tapaculo, *Scytalopus femoralis*, is the size of a large wren and similar in general form. It is a blackish-brown bird with narrow reddish scalloping. The most highly specialized tapaculo is the quail-sized Ocellated Babbler, *Acropternis orthonyx*, which has a curiously flat bridge to its rail-like bill, and tremendously elongated hind nails. It is reddish brown with black body plumes, each with a solitary round white spot.

## ANT PIPITS

The dozen or so species of this family are short-tailed, long-legged birds, very similar in appearance and habits to some of the ant birds. The ant pipits are all denizens of jungle undergrowth in the American tropics. These birds are usually gray above, whitish below with a white eyebrow of lengthened feathers and a black or chestnut cap. They differ in some respects of body structure from the ant birds; that is why they are placed in a separate family, the Conopophagidae.

## LYREBIRDS—THEY CAN IMITATE AN AUTOMOBILE HORN

Australia has many candidates for the title of the world's strangest bird. Perhaps the most unusual of the lot is the Superb Lyrebird, *Menura superba*. The cock lyrebird is a remarkable vocalist and can imitate a great many birds—and even such sounds as the honk of an automobile horn. But this bird will amaze you even before it utters a sound, for it has long lyre-shaped outer tail feathers fully two feet long. These plumes are whitish marked with V-shaped areas of deep umber brown. The whitish central tail feathers have a filmy, lacelike structure.

This magnificent tail has considerable courtship value, and the male lyrebird knows how to make the most of it. He builds an unobstructed moundlike display area on the forest floor. Then, to attract a mate near his mound, he spreads his tail to the utmost and brings it forward so that the feathers extend over his head, meanwhile calling and singing.

The nest of the lyrebird is a large, globular affair. The single heavily marked egg takes five weeks to incubate, and the development of the young is correspondingly slow.

**THE LYREBIRD AND ITS EXTRAORDINARY TAIL**

Famous for its amazingly beautiful tail feathers (their lyre shape is shown in the detail), this Australian bird is a great mimic. Observers credit it with being able to imitate the honk of an automobile horn. The lyrebird, by the way, is the largest of all the perching birds. The male shows off on a "stage" from which he has removed all forest litter.

About the size of a rooster, the lyrebird was grouped with the pheasants by early explorers because of the structure of its head and bill and its strong legs. Later on, naturalists realized that the lyrebird was a very unusual member of the order of perching birds. In fact, it is the largest bird of the order. The only other member of the lyrebird family (Menuridae) is Albert's Lyrebird, *Menura alberti*, which lacks the beautiful tail plumes. The family has no close relatives, though the rare little Australian Scrubbird, *Atrichornis*, is similar in some ways.

## SCRUBBIRDS—ANCIENT AND NEARLY EXTINCT

Living in some of the densest scrub and brush in Australia, the scrubbirds hide and skulk so well that it is almost impossible to make them fly. The birds have a very loud voice, said to be ventriloquistic. One of the two species is probably extinct, and in fact this apparently ancient group (family Atrichornithidae) is nearing complete extinction. Scrubbirds look like wrens, but they have several peculiarities of structure, such as the lack of a furculum ("wishbone").

## LARKS—ECSTATIC SONGSTERS

The lark has had perhaps more recognition from the poets than any other bird. We all know Shakespeare's "Hark! hark! the lark at Heaven's gate sings," and Coleridge likened the lark's performance to the singing of "an angel in the clouds." There is good observation as well as imagination in these descriptions, and for this reason: The lark is partial to open country and, since it lacks an elevated perch from which to sing, it mounts high into the air to pour forth its ecstatic songs.

The seventy-five species of larks make up what is primarily an Old World family, the Alaudidae. In fact, only one of them, the Horned Lark, *Otocoris alpestris*, has become firmly established in America. Like other larks, it favors open country and is therefore more common in the west than in the east—though even in the east it has become more abundant since the clearing of the forests.

The colors of the horned lark blend with soil and sand. Observe it at close range, however, and you will see that it is a pretty bird with a black collar and a yellow stripe over the eye; the back is suffused with pink. The "horns" are two little tufts of black feathers on the forehead—but these are rarely visible.

The most famous songster of the family is of course the European Skylark, *Alauda arvensis*, but the horned lark is not much inferior to it as a vocalist. Larks lay four or five mottled grayish eggs in a simple grass nest on the ground. Like many other ground birds, larks run rather than hop.

## OLD WORLD LARKS

A brownish-streaked species, the celebrated skylark has a modest garb not at all in keeping with its ranking as a songster. Widely introduced into America, it has failed to survive there, though for many years it was possible to find a few of these birds on Long Island, New York.

Many desert larks are protectively colored. Where the soil is reddish, the larks have a similar color—the same feature applies for blackish, brown, or gray soils. This adaptive camouflage is the lark's chief resource against attacks by hawks in deserts or grassy plains where there are no bushes or other cover.

## SWALLOWS—GRACEFUL, FRIENDLY AND USEFUL

Swallows are among the most attractive of all songbirds. Their flight is a byword for gracefulness as they carry on their almost incessant pursuit of flies and other insects. When the farmer mows his hayfields he is often accompanied by a group of swallows, swooping back and forth above the cutter bar to catch the insects as they are disturbed in

**THE BARN SWALLOW—MAN'S FRIEND**
Though it formerly nested on rocks, the barn swallow generally builds its nest nowadays on the walls of buildings. Like all swallows, it captures a great many insects in the course of its graceful flight. This seven-inch songster is among the tamest of wild birds.

flight. These birds have a short, flat bill with a broad gape that enables them to get the most insects for their exertions.

Over much of the United States the best known of the swallows (there are seventy-five species in the family Hirundinidae) is the Barn Swallow, *Hirundo rustica,* or Common Swallow as it is called in the Old World. Like all the other swallows, it has very small, weak legs and feet—it can perch well but rarely attempts to walk. The back of this beautiful bird is glistening bluish black, the breast reddish, and the long, forked tail is ornamented with white spots.

Once the barn swallow nested on cliffs, but now it almost invariably makes its home on ledges or on beams of barns or other buildings. Thus the barn swallow is man's friend not only because of the large quantities of insect pests it consumes, but also because of its nesting habits. The nest itself is made largely of mud and can be plastered onto any convenient wall so long as some slight support is available. After lining the nest with feathers, usually obtained from some nearby chicken yard, the barn swallow lays four or five white eggs spotted with cinnamon brown. The birds often rear two broods in a single season, and they may use the same nest year after year. Their song is a musical twittering, especially pleasing when uttered by several swallows in unison as they snuggle side by side on a beam to enjoy the first warming rays of the morning sun.

**The Cliff Swallow,** *Petrochelidon albifrons,* has also learned to nest on buildings, placing its large mud nests on the outside of barns—just below the eaves where they are protected from rain. Because of this trait it is often called the "eave swallow." A famous colony of cliff swallows has nested for years at the Mission of San Capistrano in California, reappearing each spring with the regularity that inspired the song "When the Swallows Come Back to Capistrano." Sometimes, however, weather changes affect the swallows' selection of a time for migrating. Then the schedule is upset, with the result, as the proverb has it, that "one swallow does not make a summer."

Cliff swallows build their homes in the form of large globular balls of mud with a spoutlike entrance on the side. In the West, where this bird still nests on cliffs in the less settled regions, enormous numbers of these mud-balls are sometimes found grouped tightly together on a cliff or steep river bank. You can easily identify the cliff swallow by a large orange spot on its lower back.

Another swallow that likes living in groups is the Purple Martin, *Progne subis.* Some people build large apartment-type birdhouses to provide a home for the martins, but unless a vigilant watch is kept, the birds are often turned out by those quarrelsome pests, the English sparrows. The purple martin, which is, by the way, the largest American swallow, is dark purplish blue.

**Most Prefer to Migrate.** Entirely dependent on flying insects for food, most swallows are highly migratory. However, they travel by day rather than by night as do many small birds. Their complete disappearance during the colder months accounts for a number of folklore beliefs—that they pass the winter in hibernation within a hollow tree or in the mud at the bottom of a pond.

One group hardier than most are the Tree Swallows, *Iridoprocne bicolor;* a few of these birds pass the winter even so far north as Long Island, New York. At this time of the year they eke out their diet with bayberries. Glossy steel blue above and shining white below, the tree swallow commands your attention as it skims by. It has a habit of placing its nest in a hollow stub near a pond, though it will readily make use of a birdhouse that is provided for it. When fall comes, immense numbers of tree swallows gather in marshes, or on telephone wires, shortly before they begin their southward journey.

The Rough-winged Swallow, *Stelgidopteryx rufipennis,* gets its curious name from the little file-like projections on the leading edge of the wings. This plain-colored brown species nests in a hole in a river bank. The Bank Swallow, *Riparia riparia,* has similar nesting habits, but unlike the rough-wing it lives in large colonies.

## CUCKOO SHRIKES—NEITHER CUCKOOS NOR SHRIKES

The cuckoo shrikes have a deceptive name. They are not closely related to either the cuckoos or the shrikes. It is true that in form and color they resemble some cuckoos, for most of them are slender, grayish or blackish birds, and their plumage, especially among the females, is often barred. The bill is slightly hooked and thus has some resemblance to a shrike's. "Caterpillar birds" might be a better name for these birds, as most of the sixty species of the family Campephagidae have a marked taste for caterpillars.

Among the cuckoo shrikes, the feathers of the lower back are stiffened and bristle-like. They build an open, cup-shaped nest and lay from two to five spotted eggs. Though indifferent songsters, they have loud call notes. Most of them make their home in the tropical regions of the Old World, a few getting as far as the temperate parts of eastern Asia. The three species of *Campephaga* proper dwell in Africa. The males are black with a bright-colored shoulder patch, giving them an appearance that may remind you of the American red-winged blackbird. Another African species, the Lobed Cuckoo Shrike, has small fleshy lobes on the sides of the face. Its plumage is bright yellow.

The largest cuckoo shrikes—those of the genus *Coracina*—are generally jay-sized birds with softly blended patterns of gray, black, and white. In the forested regions where they dwell they invite attention with their loud calls.

We find the Minivets, *Pericrocotus,* in India and bordering countries. They have very bright plumage—red and black or yellow and black are the predominant colors. The Ashy Minivet, *Pericrocotus roseus,* ranges as far north as Japan. In winter it migrates to the Malay countries and the Philippine Islands. At this season the birds congregate in large flocks that keep to the tops of the tall jungle trees.

## BULBULS—SOCIABLE AND NOISY

The word *bulbul* comes from the Arabic word for "nightingale," though bulbuls are not noted for melody. Many bulbuls are sociable creatures, found in pairs or flocks, and often the most common birds in the areas where they dwell. Some live in deep forest, usually near the ground, others stick to the middle and upper tiers of original tropical and subtropical forest. Still others frequent grasslands and cultivated areas, often near cattle and human habitations. There are a hundred or so species of these inconspicuous, medium-sized birds that resemble tropical flycatchers. They dwell in the warmer parts of Africa, Asia, and the Oriental region, making up the family Pycnonotidae.

All these birds have a short neck and wings, a long tail, and fine, fluffy feathers on the back and rump. The bill varies quite a bit. It may be short and cone-shaped, elongated and slender, or sharply hooked. Male and female are similarly colored—chiefly dull olive gray or brown and quite frequently washed with yellow. The bulbul feeds on fruit, berries, insects, and seeds. We are told that the South African Bulbul, *Pycnonotus tricolor*, occasionally becomes so intoxicated from feeding on syringa berries that it is easily captured by hand.

The Yellow-vented Bulbul, *Pycnonotus goiavier*, of the Philippines, Indo-China, and Malaysia, is perhaps the commonest Philippine bird in orchards and brushy areas near human habitations. About eight inches long, it has white eyebrows and brownish upper parts. Below, it is tinted with lemon yellow, particularly on the vent and under tail coverts.

In the more forested areas of the Philippines, the Philippine Bulbul, *Microscelis gularis*, is the most frequently encountered bird and, despite its dullish color, the most prominent one. It is very sociable and extremely noisy; though its call notes are loud, they are not unpleasant. In the pine forests of Okinawa a somewhat larger and related bulbul, *Microscelis amaurotis*, made itself known to the American troops by its noisy calls and inquisitive jaylike habits. Like other bulbuls it builds a simple, cuplike nest in a tree or bush and lays a few spotted eggs.

## FAIRY BLUEBIRDS AND LEAFBIRDS—ZOO FAVORITES

Many of the sixteen species of this small family are favorites in zoos and aviaries. Related to the bulbuls to some extent, they are usually brighter in color and differ in other ways as well. They are at home in the tropical parts of Asia, the Philippines, and the East Indies.

The Fairy Bluebirds, *Irena*, are brilliant birds, glistening blue with black marks. The Leafbirds, *Chloropsis*, are also brightly colored, but green and yellow or orange are their main colors. The members of the Irenidae family, the fairy bluebirds as well as the leafbirds, live on fruit and, to a lesser extent, insects. Their nests, which they place in a tree, are open, cuplike structures.

## MOCKINGBIRDS, THRASHERS, AND CATBIRDS

"Listen to the mockingbird!" the song goes, and you will find the advice well worth taking. Unmatched as a vocalist, the mockingbird has a haunting song that it pours out as it perches on the ridgepole of a cabin in the southland. With a rich repertoire of songs of its own, the mockingbird also mimics almost every other bird and frog found in its neighborhood. With equal ease it negotiates the sparrow's chirping, the swallow's twittering, the crow's cawing, the whippoorwill's strident call, and even the scream of the hawk.

**"LISTEN TO THE MOCKINGBIRD!"**
The mockingbird is adept at imitating the whippoorwill, crow, hawk, and many other birds—so much so that we easily forget that it has a very beautiful song of its own. However, as far as looks are concerned, this superlative songster is anything but striking.

**The Mockingbird,** *Mimus polyglottos* ("many tongues"), is by far the most famous of this New World family, the Mimidae, which contains thirty species. Slender birds with long tails and short, rounded wings, they are partial to dense brush. There is nothing in the mockingbird's appearance to give you a hint of its superb song—it is merely a gray and white bird of robin size. Common throughout the South, it is the state bird of Florida, Mississippi, Tennessee, Arkansas, and Texas.

**The Brown Thrasher,** *Toxostoma rufum,* like all other members of this family, frequents dense brush; but when it is about to sing it mounts to the top of a tall bush or tree, and that is the best time for you to watch it. An excellent songster, it rarely mimics other birds. A distinctive feature of its song is the repetition of each phrase.

The brown thrasher, a long-tailed bird with reddish-brown and white plumage, is the only thrasher found in the eastern United States. Two or three other kinds make their home in the desert areas of southwestern North America. They have sandy-colored plumage—useful in such surroundings—and they dig for food in loose sand with their long, curved bills. As they dig, they often swing the head from side to side. Although the brown thrasher has a very short singing season, we have found the Crissal Thrasher, *Toxostoma dorsale,* still singing its somewhat similar song as late as November in Sonora, Mexico. These long-legged birds spend much time on the ground. They are shy and make off rapidly in the thorny desert brush whenever they are disturbed.

**The Catbird,** *Dumetella carolinensis,* one of the commonest birds of the United States, has a petulant, scolding note very similar to the *meow* of a cat. The catbird's song, if we may call it that, is a squeaky, grating travesty of the songs of the mockingbird and thrasher. Yet the catbird is closely related to the thrashers and has similar habits. It has deep slaty gray plumage with a chestnut area under the tail. Its range is more northern than the mockingbird's.

Like other members of this family, the catbird builds a cup-shaped nest placed in dense bushes. Its eggs are unspotted greenish blue, while those of the mockingbird and of most thrashers are spotted.

## WRENS—SOME ARE CAVE DWELLERS

Wrens are small, chunky, energetic birds with a rather long tail usually held straight above the back, giving them a pert air. Related to the thrashers and thrushes, wrens have wings that are short and rounded at the tips.

**The Winter Wren,** *Troglodytes troglodytes,* is the only Old World wren, and one of the smallest of the sixty-odd species of the family Troglodytidae. The term "troglodyte" (cave dweller) alludes to the liking of this wren for creeping about, almost like a mouse, in dark recesses beneath river banks or among the roots of overturned trees. As its common name tells us, the winter wren is hardier than the other members of the family, which are mostly confined to the warmer regions of America. It was through this partiality for more northern latitudes that the winter wren was able to enter the Old World from America via Alaska and Siberia.

Like its cousins, this wren has a melodious, bubbling song. Its nest is a globular ball of moss, with an entrance hole on the side. It lays six or eight tiny speckled eggs. Like all other wrens, this bird feeds on insects and their eggs.

**The House Wren,** *Troglodytes aedon,* **is** as apt as not to change mates for each of the two or three broods raised during a season. At least that was the conclusion reached from a study of the "marriage relations" of the house wren, conducted in Ohio. It would seem that no lasting ties develop between mates, and if one of them is impelled by an urge to begin a nesting cycle before the other, a change of mates is likely to take place.

The house wren is a familiar bird in most parts of the United States. If you put up a small birdhouse in your backyard, you may have a "Jenny Wren" as a summer guest. The male utters his bubbling song incessantly—it has been counted as much as six thousand times in a single day. When a birdhouse is not available to a pair, they nest, like their ancestors, in a natural cavity in a stub. The nest, built of twigs, is surprisingly bulky. Wrens are rather intolerant of other small birds, and they are believed to puncture the eggs of other birds on occasion.

**The Cactus Wren,** *Heleodytes brunneicapillus* ("brown-cap"), dwells in the southwestern American deserts. About the size of a catbird, it is much larger than most of its cousins. Its plumage is a checkered pattern of browns, grays, and buffs. In appearance the cactus wren is not unlike a small thrasher, but its grating and churring call notes are distinctly wrenlike. The nest of the cactus wren is a large, globe-shaped mass of sticks lined with grass and placed in some cactus or spiny mesquite bush where it is safe from most enemies.

Some tropical wrens are so furtive that it is almost impossible to observe them. At such times we must content ourselves with listening to their vocal accomplishments. Occasionally we can hear a pair of wrens sing a duet, uttering alternate notes in perfect timing.

# Ants, Bees, Spiders and Worms

---

### ANTS—COLONISTS, WORKERS, AND WARRIORS

Ants, like beetles, are almost easier to find than to elude. You see ants on lawns, roadways, and city pavements; in gardens, forests, and pastures. These extraordinary insects vary in size and color from the big carpenter ant to the little brown species that is the most common of all in North America. There are many localities where you may find this brown ant; but because it has been studied chiefly in cornfields, it is widely known as the "cornfield ant."

*Ant Colonies:* The cornfield ant, like all members of the ant family, lives in colonies. Each colony is made up of three principal types of ants: the queen (or fertile female) ; the short-lived males that die soon after the mating flight; and the infertile females. These last, the great majority, are the ordinary hard working citizens of the ant world. They are divided into workers, soldiers, or other specialized castes. The workers have larger heads and part of their front legs is slightly thicker than in other adults of this species.

If you come upon a mound of earth about which ants are hustling, your youngster may exclaim, "There's an anthill!" And if he is of an adventurous turn of mind, he may want to dig into it to see just what an ant colony is like. But in order to examine

233

a nest successfully, you have to dig down with great skill—else you may merely ruin it.

*Inside the Ant Colony:* Observe the nests of cornfield ants closely and you will realize that these nests vary greatly in size. The mound of a long-established colony covers a much larger area than that of a new one. As a rule, the underground rooms are only a few inches below the surface. But after a long dry spell, or if the nest is located in sandy soil, the rooms are deeper in the earth; for soil that is very dry becomes too crumbly for excavation.

In the winter you would find the apartments occupied only by inactive adults and larvae. In midsummer the rooms bulge with eggs, larvae, pupae, workers, males and females. (The eggs are tiny specks.) The larvae are white maggot-like creatures, and the pupae are enclosed in whitish cocoons about an eighth of an inch long. Often mistakenly called "ant eggs," the pupae are collected in large numbers and sold as fish and bird food.

*How Ant Life is Organized:* If you were to discover an ant nest on a fine afternoon in August or early September, you might find the occupants swarming excitedly about the entrance; you might also notice that many of them have wings. Every few minutes a winged form takes to the air. Some of these are males, some females. (Apparently their mating takes place in the air.)

When the female returns to the ground she breaks off her wings, then burrows a few inches into the earth or finds an opening beneath a log or stone. Here she forms a small cell. She may then immediately start to lay her eggs—or she may wait until the following spring. As time goes on she eats some of the eggs—they are the only food she has—and continues to lay more. About two months after she begins to raise her young she may have one or two workers.

During the first year, if she does well, her colony increases to about twenty-five adult workers. Their duty is to search far and wide for her food. They feed her and the larvae as well, also helping the larvae to spin their cocoons and in time assisting the new adults as they escape from these cocoons. Their mandibles and forelegs make excellent tools. With these, too, they dig out new tunnels and rooms; and as they dig and bring soil up to the surface of the ground, the "anthill" grows larger. When the soil becomes cold, they close the entrance to the nest and rest quietly in the rooms until the next spring.

*Savage Ant Warriors:* Not all ants are as settled in their ways as the cornfield ant. There are some that do not bother to build homes at all: They are almost constantly on the move, wandering from place to place in search of food. Among these nomads are the "driver" ants of Africa and tropical America. They march in close formation, in columns an inch or two wide and sometimes a mile long! Even animals as large as a deer will flee in terror from such an army.

## GRASSHOPPERS AND THEIR MUSIC

*Katydids—Fiddlers, Not Singers:* Katydids have become so closely identified with this name because of their insistent refrain *Katy did, no she didn't,* that people sometimes forget these insects are also grasshoppers. The grasshoppers are divided into two groups: the short- and long-horned families. The "horns" (really the antennae) are considered long if they are nearly as long as, or longer than, the insect's body. Katydids belong to the long-horned group.

A child hearing them on a summer night may refer to their "singing," but "fiddling" is a better word for their kind of music. A male katydid—the females only listen—rubs its left wing over the right wing. The left wing has a file-like row of ridges, while the right wing has a hard little scraper just behind the shoulder where the wings overlap; the rubbing of the wings produces the fiddling sound.

*Fiddlers All:* It is the broad-winged or leaf-winged katydid that plays its name with insistent repetition. The large oblong-winged tree katydid has a refrain of *Zzzzzz-Ipswich;* the fork-tailed bush katydid plays a slow *zeep-zeep-zeep* now and then; and the common meadow katydid fiddles several soft *zees* in a row, each faster than the one before, and then hits and holds a high *zeee.*

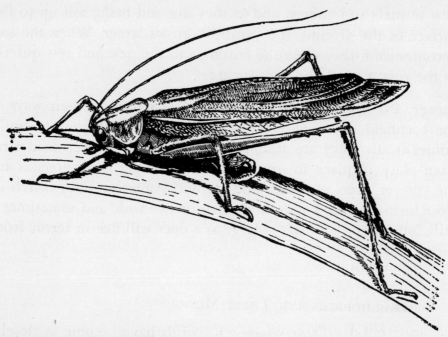

**"KATY DID — NO SHE DIDN'T"**
The katydids are long-horned grasshoppers noted for their fondness for fiddling.
The sound is produced by rubbing the left wing over the right wing. The males
do all the playing, while the females are apparently content to listen. The katydid
has hearing organs on its front legs.

A short-horned grasshopper has a different fiddling technique. Its long hind leg forms the bow, and a coarse outer wing the fiddle. It may play one leg and wing at a time or both sides together—a "one-man duet." However, little actual music is created by these efforts; you can hear the resulting rasps for only a few feet.

Both males and females have large hearing organs. You can see what looks like an oval window on each side of the first abdominal segment under the wings. What you see is the outer part of the grasshopper's "ears."

Grasshoppers blend so successfully with their surroundings that it is not easy to spot them during the day except when they take wing. Some of the smaller katydids are easily startled into flight from tall weeds and grasses where they spend much of their time. In the country you can have a lively evening tracking down the little insect fiddlers; take a flashlight along and let yourself be guided by their sounds.

*Crickets Join the Insect Serenade:* The chirpy, cheerful cricket produces music with its wings in the same way as the katydid, but usually with its right wing over the left—whereas the katydid, as we have seen, rubs its left wing over the right. To a listening youngster it may seem that the katydids dominate the insect serenade; but crickets contribute their share of the melodious performance. The tune of the common snowy tree cricket begins as a musical *waa-waa-waa*, played by individuals, each "on his own." But soon they join forces and play as if they were following a conductor's baton.

*Crickets As Weather Forecasters:* The performance of the snowy tree cricket is directly related to the temperature. By counting the number of notes it produces each minute, you can roughly gauge what your thermometer registers. Thus, a hundred chirps to the minute indicate a temperature of 63 degrees. Increasing its tempo as the temperature rises, this cricket slows down when it gets cooler.

The common black crickets, with their clear chirp, are the first musicians you will hear in summer. You may often discover them, by late August, if you turn over an old board or stone. They run fast but despite their muscular-looking legs they do not imitate the grasshopper's high-jumping tactics.

*Cricket on the Hearth:* The cricket that may serenade you from indoors after cool weather begins is not necessarily the same kind about which Dickens wrote so appealingly in England; but the American field cricket is also a cheery visitor to have on the hearth. The European cricket is now quite well established in the eastern United States and is a persistent fiddler. Unfortunately, once these musicians are indoors they do not limit their activities to music but may get into food and eat holes in everything made of cloth.

*How To Keep Cricket Pets:* In the natural state, not many crickets survive the coming of frost. However, if they are adopted as pets, they will often live through the winter with every appearance of enjoying themselves. You can make a cage for a cricket very simply with a flowerpot full of earth and a kerosene lamp chimney.

Sink the chimney into the earth to a depth of two inches and cover the top with a piece of mosquito netting held in place by a rubber band. You can make a similar cage with a large jar, or an aquarium also covered with mosquito netting, and with soil and plants set on the bottom.

Once you have obtained a few crickets, place them inside the cage with a cabbage leaf or other greens and fasten the mosquito netting top. Aside from providing their leafy food, it is a good idea to occasionally drop a little corn meal saturated with water into the glass cage—it will furnish moisture as well as food. Periodically, too, the inside quarters should be sprinkled with water to keep the atmosphere moist.

You may conclude from sad experience that it is not practicable to keep more than one cricket in the cage; they frequently start fighting with fatal results.

### Bees—Honey-Makers, Pollinizers, and Stingers

What probably impresses children above all about bees is their stinging ability. "Is it true that a bee dies after it stings you? Can only females sting? Don't bees sting when they are swarming?" I have heard youngsters put these queries incessantly before the topic of honey-making ever came up.

*The Bee's Sting:* Tormenting humans is far from the primary use of stingers. When the first queen hatches in a hive, she immediately rips open other queen cells—unless she is restrained by the workers—and stings the inmates to death, thereby removing all possible rivals. Queens have the ability to sting over and over again—but they use their sting only on other queens.

It is a worker bee that will sting you, and it commits suicide by doing so. Stinging brings twenty-two muscles into play; when the stinger is torn out of the worker's body, death results.

The order of insects to which bees—and wasps and ants—belong is the only one in which genuine stingers are found. The stinger is the modified ovipositor (or egg-laying organ) of the female worker, so obviously the males or "drones" possess no stings. In early summer, when a mass of bees leave their hive with a queen

to found a new home, they seem especially tolerant of bystanders
and almost never sting during this swarming.

*Very Few Kinds of Bees Store Honey:* Many children and even
some grownups have a mistaken idea that all bees store honey.
Actually this is true of only a few of the thousands of kinds of
bees known to exist. Most of them eat nectar as they take it from
the flowers, instead of using it for honey.

The true honeybees, so valuable in fertilizing such plants as
clover and fruit trees, are native to Europe; they were introduced
to North America by colonists in the seventeenth century. If you
find any of these in hollow trees in the woods, they are swarms
that have escaped from man-made hives—or descendants of such
bees.

*The Underground Bumblebee:* The large, hairy bumblebee, with
its black coat marked with yellow, orange, or red, is probably
more quickly recognized by children than most species. This
honey manufacturer is native to America. Bumblebees live in
large colonies underground, where they construct many-celled
combs. In the cells they lay eggs, store pollen and nectar, and
make honey.

*Playing Bee Detective:* Country youngsters have long delighted in
tracking down honeybees that have "gone native," and finding
their store of honey. The bee detective's equipment is a small box
with either honey or sugar water and an opening large enough to
enable the bees to get to it. The same purpose is achieved by
using one of those frames in which honey is bought in the comb.
Putting some flour or cornstarch in the receptacle will give the
bees a touch of white as they take the bait. Thus they will be
more conspicuous at a distance, making it possible to follow the
direction of their flight.

Your bee detective places the box on a stump or post in a
neighborhood where bees are working. By moving the box at
intervals in the direction of their flight, the youthful hunter
gradually narrows down the distance to the bees' storehouse.

The first customers will usually bring other workers with them.
Individual bees can be identified after a while, and the lessening

time required to complete the round trip will indicate how much the distance to the hive is decreasing. Although the youngster will be overjoyed when he finally locates the store of honey, it is a wise precaution to have him call on adult help in removing the honey from the hollow-tree storehouse.

*How Bees Use "Glue":* When you see a bee purposefully visiting tree after tree, it may be gathering water from the buds. The other object of its quest may be a brown resinous material—called "propolis" or "bee glue"—that these insects use for smoothing rough places in the hive. This assignment is given to young bees on their first flights.

*Pollination by Messenger Service:* Later on, the bees set about collecting pollen and finally nectar. They knead the pollen into a little ball and tuck it into a cavity on the hind leg; they obtain nectar by extending their tongue into a flower and sucking the fluid. There are some species of clovers and other plants with long-tubed corollas that depend completely on bumblebees and other long-tongued species of bees for pollination.

Western fruitgrowers keep colonies of bees in the great orchards for fertilizing the fruit-tree blooms. (Some owners rent the bees for this purpose.) Honeybees are more valuable to man in this way than they are as producers of honey and beeswax.

*What Goes On In A Beehive:* Many children are familiar with the beehives provided by people to keep bee colonies and to take advantage of the bees' honey production. This kind of hive usually has one lower story, in which the frames are used both for the brood and for storing honey which the bees use in winter. There are one or more upper stories with additional frames for storing honey.

As they would do in a natural hive, the bees house their brood in the lower section, then work hard filling the top part with honey. Beekeepers remove the upper frames as they are filled. Small sections of each frame, containing about a pound of honey, are taken out in the form you buy them in at the store. The honey is removed from the larger frames and sold in liquid form.

*How Bees Make Honeycombs:* To store honey, honeybees manufacture cells from wax produced by certain glands in their bodies. (Bumblebees do this also. Many species make their cells of wood, leaves, or earth.)

The making of a honeybee comb is an amazing example of co-operative effort. A group of bees begin by forming a living curtain of their bodies, each one holding on with its forefeet to the hind feet of the bee above. After they have remained in that position for some time, little plates of wax appear on each insect's abdomen. They then chew the wax and form it into a comb.

*The Bee's "Honey Stomach":* The nectar that the bees take from flowers becomes honey in the insects' "honey stomach." This organ is not involved in ordinary digestion; the nectar is mixed in the honey stomach with secretions from glands that cause chemical changes. The cane sugar of nectar, for example, turns into the fruit sugar of honey—a form that we can digest more readily.

*Money From Honey:* Keeping honeybees is a hobby that may be made to pay dividends. Some people are successful at housing them in relatively small back yards, so long as there are nearby meadows to which the insects can fly. Bees need comparatively little care, but before you purchase a swarm or hive, you will do well to seek advice either directly from an expert or from literature on the subject.

## Some Unpopular Insects

### WASPS—CLEVER PAPERMAKERS

Proud indeed is the young nature collector who can add a hornet's nest to his home exhibits. It is a real showpiece—an impressive example of the skill of the insects often claimed to be the cleverest of the entire six-footed tribe.

The bald-faced hornet is one of several wasps that manufacture paper by chewing bits of wood to a pulp and use it to construct nests sometimes massive in size. Some wasps—like the hornet—suspend the nest from a branch of a tree or bush, while others attach their homes to eaves or barn roofs—or locate them in cavities in the ground or in tree trunks.

*How the Wasp Builds Its Paper Nest:* If you observe these wasps when they are busy with their home construction, you will see them flying off in search of weathered wood or cut wood fibers in a post, an unpainted old building, or a piece of a dead tree trunk. From something of this sort, a wasp builder bites and tears the fiber with its mandibles, taking enough to form a pellet about an eighth of an inch across the middle. It tucks the pellet under its chin and chews until the wood is sufficiently turned into a mass of doughy pulp.

**STYLES IN WASP ARCHITECTURE**

When wasps are mentioned, most of us immediately think of their stinging habits. Actually, their abilities as builders are far more remarkable. The "paper" wasp (upper left) chews wood into paper pulp for its nest. The mud-dauber wasps (right) mix mud and saliva to mortar their nests.

The insect now returns to the nest and, alighting astride an unfinished layer of paper, presses down the new ball of pulp, biting it to fasten it in place. Then the wasp walks slowly backward, unraveling the ball and fastening it to the layer of paper below. When the new pulp is all laid out, the wasp runs forward, then once more backs up, biting the pulp all along the way to flatten it. While the moisture is drying out, the wasp is off collect‐ ing more fiber. As these fibers are collected from a variety of sources, the color of the paper may vary in different parts of the nest!

It is usually safe to watch bald-faced hornets or yellow jackets —which are also papermakers—at work as long as you do not disturb them. But if you poke into their nest or meddle with their activities, you will quickly discover the origin of the phrase, "mad as a hornet."

*Wasp Homes of Mud:* Paper nests are not the only kind built by wasps. Your observant youngster may come across cartridge-shaped cells made of mud and attached to the walls of garages, barns, or other buildings—as well as many out-of-the-way "unlikely" places. Such cells are constructed by mud-dauber wasps.

At first there is only one cell, about an inch long; but soon an‐ other is added next to it, and before the builder is finished there may be half a dozen more. On a hot summer day you may catch sight of these wasps collecting little balls of mud at the side of a puddle of water. You can even set up an observation post by forming a mud puddle there.

### THE WOOD-EATING TERMITES

Most children know about these notorious insects, and the damage they do to wooden structures; but few people get to see these creatures. Termites live in the dark seclusion of tunnels, and the first intimation of their presence may come when a fence falls down or a wooden step gives way. (They have also been known to eat through table tops and window frames!)

The one time you are likely to see them in the light of day is on the occasion of the marriage flight of a colony. Then swarms of these insects—the male and female winged forms—may emerge from walls, porch supports, or anywhere near the wood founda‐ tions of a house.

Though termites are often called "white ants," they belong to an entirely different order of insects. It is easy to recognize them by their shape; termites are broad where the thorax and abdomen join. They do not have the indentation or "waist" that all ants have. The worker and soldier termites are almost colorless and blind. The winged females and males, the future queens and kings of new colonies, are dark-colored and have eyes. Actually termites are more closely related to roaches than to ants.

*How Termites Digest Wood:* Nearly any child can tell you that termites "eat wood," but few of us are aware of the strange alliance that makes it possible for them to live on this "food." Each termite harbors numerous tiny one-celled animals that break down the cellulose content of wood into digestible substances. If you were to place a termite in a temperature high enough to kill its minute parasites, it might continue to eat wood but would derive no nourishment; before long it would die of starvation!

### FLIES—CARRIERS OF DISEASE

We all dislike and mistrust flies. They are generally targets for destruction rather than objects of study. But despite all our efforts to wipe them out, they are so extraordinarily successful in surviving that they become objects of interest for that very reason. There are many species of flies, but probably the most familiar—perhaps the most familiar of all insects—is the common housefly.

*A Generation A Month:* The difficulty of keeping houseflies in check is easy to understand once we are aware of the rate at which they produce their young. The female lays a mass of from twenty-five to about a hundred eggs at a time. In less than a day these hatch into tiny white maggots about as large as the point of a pin. The maggots—actually larvae—mature in four or five days, then enter the pupa stage which lasts another five days or so. The full-grown fly now appears.

Shortly after, the mother of this brood may lay another mass of eggs; and the new generation begins producing young of its own within a few days after becoming adults. As long as warm weather lasts, generations follow each other from within two weeks to a month.

The arrival of cold weather destroys the adult flies, eggs, and larvae. The pupae in their protective shells survive, remaining inactive during the winter. With the onset of warm weather they quickly complete their development, and the same process begins all over again. The average life of an adult is from two to three weeks; some live considerably longer.

*The Fly's Cleaning Routine:* If you have ever watched a fly cleaning itself, you must have wondered at its reputation for filthiness. Its grooming is remarkably thorough. First it rubs its front feet together briskly so that the hairs on one leg act as a brush for the other leg, then the fly nibbles at the front feet with the rasping disk it has in lieu of teeth.

Next the creature gives its whole head an energetic scrubbing with its clean front feet. It pulls forward its middle pair of legs, one at a time, and brushes and nibbles them. Finally its hind feet are used to clean each other and to brush its wings and most of its body.

All this careful grooming is deceptive, however, as far as protecting our health is concerned. Flies breed in manure and the odors of fermented or decayed plants and animals have a special attraction for them. Harmful germs cling to their feet and are deposited in food on which they may alight. Typhoid fever and amebic dysentery are among the many diseases they are known to spread. It is true that many kinds of flies render important service as scavengers and exterminators of other objectionable insects; but credit is given them grudgingly,if it is given at all, because their relatives are so unpopular.

*The Fly's Wing Structure:* Flies differ from most other adult insects in having a single pair of wings instead of two pairs. (Dragonflies, mayflies and others with four wings are not really flies.) Nevertheless they seem able to keep flying indefinitely, as you will notice when you chase one with a swatter. Hind wings are replaced by short stalks, or knobs, which are important in balancing them as they fly.

*How Flies Walk Upside Down:* You can observe, too, how a fly crawls up walls, windows, and across a ceiling as easily as it walks across the floor. Two tiny claws on the last segment of each foot aid it in walking on rough surfaces. It also has on each foot two small flat pads covered on the lower side with tiny hairs. These hairs give out a sticky fluid which effectively holds the insect on slippery surfaces and upside-down positions. It is these hairs that retain the great number of germs carried by flies.

### BLOODTHIRSTY MOSQUITOES

As in the case of the bee's sting, the feature of the mosquito that chiefly interests children is this insect's bite. But while many bees are highly useful to man, little but trouble can be expected from mosquitoes. In the humid tropics they are the dreaded carriers of such diseases as malaria and yellow fever. The relatively harmless and very abundant salt-marsh mosquitoes of the Atlantic and Gulf coasts inflict painful bites but do not transmit disease.

The female mosquitoes, like the female bees, are the trouble-makers; the female of most species has piercing-sucking mouth parts and its thirst for blood makes it a great pest for man and beast. Some males have an elongated "beak," but it is not suited for piercing skin. They live on the juices of fruits and plants. It is the females, too, that "sing" by vibrating thin hard projections that lie across their breathing pores.

*How Mosquito Eggs Develop:* Mosquito eggs can hatch only in water. Even small puddles are good breeding grounds. Where eggs have been laid on dry land, a hard rain may provide sufficient moisture for them to develop. The water must remain standing long enough—from two to three weeks—for egg, larva, and pupa stages to be completed if an adult is to emerge. If a puddle dries up in less time, the insects die.

A female mosquito lays a mass of from fifty to several hundred eggs. The larvae that develop from these eggs are aptly known as "wrigglers." The pupae, or "tumblers," are also lively in the water and move about lashing their tail-like abdomens. Though they require no food, they must have air, and frequently come to the surface of the water to inhale through their short breathing tubes.

*Crane Flies:* Often a child believes that he has discovered a giant mosquito when he sees a long-legged, gangling creature awkwardly drifting through the air. The chances are it is a crane fly—an absolutely harmless insect. In spring and autumn you may see large swarms of crane flies dancing a few feet above the ground or water.

## The Dragonfly—Beautiful, and Useful Too

### "DEVIL'S DARNING NEEDLE" AND OTHER NICKNAMES

Though the dragonfly is one of the most beautiful of all insects, and harmless as well, it may terrify a small child who has heard some of its nicknames and the old fables in which they originated. "Devil's darning needle" recalls the old superstition that this insect can sew up children's ears; "mule-killer" reminds us that the dragonfly was once believed to kill livestock. The name "snake-doctor" was inspired by the weird notion that it brought dead water snakes to life.

*An Underlip With Claws:* However, "mosquito hawk" *is* a well-deserved title, for dragonflies in their nymphal stage (spent in water) eat quantities of mosquito larvae. As an adult, a dragonfly catches all sorts of insects on the wing—flies, honeybees, butterflies, and sometimes other dragonflies smaller than itself. The nymph has a long underlip that folds back between its front legs. When it approaches a victim this lower lip shoots out rapidly and grasps the prey with two claws that form a pair of pincers at its end. Though it is a serious threat to mosquitoes and other insects, the dragonfly neither stings nor bites people.

*The Metamorphosis of the Dragonfly:* If yours is a family of early risers, you may some day thrill to the memorable sight of a dragonfly emerging from its nymph. You would have to go exploring along the edge of a pond about six o'clock of a summer morning and watch carefully for one of the grotesque nymphs crawling out of the water, up a tree trunk, water plant, or other support.

Sure of its support, it now strains at its armor-like covering until the skin of its back splits along its length; then very carefully it begins to pull its soft body from the shell. When this has been accomplished, the two pairs of transparent, glistening wings expand and harden. Sometimes these wings are beautifully tinted in blue and brown. The insect has an elongated body, and its great, compound eyes cover almost the entire surface of its head.

*The Damsel Fly:* It is quite a puzzle to distinguish the dragonfly from its close relative the damsel fly. They are alike in many ways, but the dragonflies have larger bodies and are stronger fliers. Also, the dragonfly always holds its wings outstretched when resting, whereas a damsel fly holds its wings together over its back.

## Insects that Live in the Water

### THE WHIRLIGIG—"LUCKY BUG"

Summer outings are a lot more fun for your children if they can make the acquaintance of some of the odd little creatures found in ponds and streams. One of the most easily observed is the whirligig, a dark, small beetle. You may see the whirligig spinning or skating in circles on the surface of the water. It is known by such charming nicknames as "lucky bug," "submarine chaser," and "write-my-name."

Usually you find whirligigs in groups, sometimes made up of hundreds of individuals. If they are alarmed, they make a sudden dive to the bottom. They prefer shade to bright sunshine and may sometimes be found out of water, resting on sticks or rocks.

The whirligig's eyes are worth special notice; each is divided so that the upper half looks into the air while the lower part looks down into the water! Its legs are also specialized, the middle and hind ones being broad and oarlike, while the front pair are long and slender. Another strange feature of the whirligig is that if you hold one in your hand for a time, you will find it gives off a white milky fluid with a smell recalling that of ripe apples.

This accounts for such local names as "apple bug" and "vanilla bug."

### THE SPEEDY WATER STRIDER

Water striders, usually found in fresh or brackish water, have very long slender middle and hind legs. It is difficult to capture them, as they skate away with great speed. The middle pair of legs propel this bug over the water while the hind pair steer. Its color is a dull dark brown above, with a silvery-white underside.

### THE UPSIDE-DOWN BUG

Another water insect, the back swimmer, is named for its habit of swimming on its back, which is shaped like the bottom of a canoe. You may first notice it as it hangs head downward in the water; but when it is alarmed, it propels itself swiftly away —bottom side up!—pushing with its hind legs.

The more common species are about half an inch long, and have enormous compound eyes. The back, which you do not see when they are swimming, is pearly-colored; the underside, which you do see, is darker. The back swimmer is easily confused with the water boatman, which is quite similar in appearance; but the boatman is smaller and never swims on its back. All these bugs, with the exception of some wingless water striders, fly at night and are strongly attracted to lights.

### THE CADDIS FLY AND ITS PROTECTIVE COVERING

Among the fascinating population of ponds and streams there are some creatures which, like the dragonfly, spend their early life in the water and then, as adults, proceed to live on land and in the air. Look in shallow pools for one of the most interesting of these. At first you may see what appears to be a stick, one or two inches long and half an inch around. If it starts to move itself along the bottom or up the stem of a plant, you know it is "animal" rather than "vegetable."

This is the larva of a small mothlike insect called the caddis fly. Many caddis fly larvae make cases of pebbles, sticks, or other materials, as a protective covering for their caterpillar-like bodies. Those that use sticks are said to construct "log cabins." More commonly they use sand or bits of vegetable matter which adhere to their bodies with silk produced by certain glands.

**THE CADDIS FLY — NATURE'S MASTER BUILDER**
In the larval stage this small mothlike insect, living at the bottom of a pond or stream, builds a case about itself from bits of plants or pebbles. (Both types are pictured underwater.) The cases, held together with gluelike silk provided by the creature's secretions, are remarkable for their skillful construction.

Still another interesting product of some caddis worms is a silken net. The insect anchors this so that the cup-shaped interior faces upstream. Thus the net serves both as protection against the current and as a food trap for the caddis worm that fashioned it.

The caddis fly emerges from its pupal form in a manner different from that of most water insects. The usual way is for them to leave the water before they attain adult form; but the caddis fly emerges at the bottom of the stream and swims to the surface.

There it usually grasps some object, climbs on it and waits for its wings to dry.

*The Fisherman's Friend:* A knowledge of these interesting insects is of practical value to the child or grown-up who wishes to do "fly-fishing" in ponds and streams. As part of this fascinating sport the fisherman uses nymphs, "wet flies," and "dry flies" to duplicate the caddis fly in all its stages. He may make these with such materials as bits of feather and hair; but even if he buys them commercially, he ought to have a knowledge of the fly and its habits in order to make the best use of his bait.

One of the most enjoyable ways for a child to observe the activities and development of water insects is to have an insect aquarium. You can keep a few specimens in jars or buckets; but a rectangular glass aquarium, which is available at a pet store, makes a much better home because you can reproduce the creatures' natural surroundings in miniature.

## Insect Oddities

### The Galls—Weird Homemakers

Insects provide many of nature's most remarkable oddities. You have discovered one of them when you observe a curious "bump" or ball on a plant stem or flower, reminding you of a large nut growing on a tree branch or leaf. It may be greenish, brown, pink, or red. If you were to cut open one of these bumps, you would discover an insect larva at its center. This identifies it as a "gall," the home of a growing creature that will develop into a small wasp, fly, or moth.

The young nature observer is likely to be puzzled by the imprisoned larva. "How does it get in there? I don't see any opening from the outside."

*How a Gall Insect Develops:* Actually, the larva doesn't "get in"; its home grows about it! Let us follow the life cycle of one of the common gall insects—a very small wasp responsible for the "oak apple." In early spring we see it deposit its eggs on the leaf of a scarlet oak. When one of these eggs develops into a legless and almost colorless larva, we note an immediate change in the leaf. Vegetable fibers start to grow, radiating out from the little grub. As this process goes on, a thin smooth crust forms around the outer edges.

Now the "oak apple" is formed, and the insect larva is completely surrounded by food and protected by its globular house. Here it eats, completes its growth, changes to a pupa, and at last emerges as a wasp, no more than a quarter-inch in length.

*Remarkable Types of Galls:* The "apple oak" is but one of the many kinds of galls. Thus, you may frequently see two different types on goldenrod stems. One of them, made by a grub that becomes a fly, is spherical in shape; the other, which is spindle-shaped, develops into a tiny moth.

Then there are the willow cone galls, produced by a little gnat. It lays its eggs on the tip of the bud of a twig. This stops the further growth of the twig, stunting the leaves into small scales which overlap in rows around the larva. The very pretty galls which you may find on wild rosebushes somewhat resemble small chestnut burs but are pink and green when young. Later they turn brown.

*Collecting Galls:* In wintertime, collecting galls makes a fine outdoor activity. Many of them are dead and deserted by then, to be sure; but in some the grubs are still resting and waiting for the onset of warm weather. The collector will find it rewarding to compare styles. A gall may be large or small, globular or spindle-shaped; its covering may be smooth, shingled, or spiny. You can succeed in identifying the insect builder once you become familiar with these variations and the kinds of plants that each insect characteristically chooses.

### THE INTERESTINGLY NAMED ANT LIONS

The larva of the ant lion, one of nature's most remarkable oddities, catches its prey in a trap. It is fairly easy to find the traps it builds, for ant lions live on sandy stretches over most of the United States and southern Canada. As in the case of the gall insects, the adult forms are undistinguished; it is the larvae, often called doodlebugs, that attract our attention.

*The Doodlebug's Ambush Technique:* The doodlebug, plump-bodied and hairy, is less than an inch long. Its head is small in proportion to its body—but its jaws are enormous in relation to the size of its head! It digs a pit in sandy or powdery soil by shoveling the earth on its head and then with a sharp jerk, throwing it a considerable distance. As it digs, it walks around and around, always *backwards,* in ever-widening circles.

Finally a tiny crater is formed, an inch and a half across or smaller, with the doodlebug buried at the bottom. With only its head and powerful jaws exposed, it waits for an ant or some other insect to slip over the edge and slide down. Then it seizes the victim, makes it helpless by injecting a paralyzing secretion into it, sucks the juice from its body, and flips the lifeless remains out of the pit by an upward jerk of its long jaws.

*How to Find Doodlebugs:* You may be interested in observing this extraordinary example of how a "lowly" creature can capture its prey by an ingenious trapping technique. You can catch a doodlebug by finding its crater and scooping your hand under to bring the insect-excavator to the surface. Place it in a box of sandy soil and you will quickly see it set to work. If you wish to see the final act of the drama, you must place ants or other insects in the box so the doodlebug will not vainly lie in wait.

### THE STRANGE PRAYING MANTIDS

I know of one little girl to whom the praying mantis will always seem curious if only because of the way she first became acquainted with this insect. On an August evening a mantis alighted on a window sill of her New York apartment! It would be hard to imagine a more unlikely intruder in such a place than this queer green creature with its pointed, elfin face and big round eyes.

The little girl managed to get it into a box and took it to the American Museum of Natural History in New York in the belief that she had something on the order of a visitor from Mars. There she learned the true nature of her captive, and also that it was quite possible to keep a mantis as a pet.

*The Preying Habits of the Praying Mantis:* In natural surroundings mantids are great hunters, capturing by stealth such lively insects as butterflies, mosquitoes, grasshoppers, beetles, and flies. The mantis lies in wait with its front legs upraised in a prayerful pose, and when its prey comes near, it snatches at the victim with lightning speed. The prey has slight chance of escaping the rows of sharp spines on the second and third joints of the mantis forelegs.

**"MULE-KILLERS" AND "DEVIL'S HORSES"**

These are some of the epithets that have been applied to the praying mantis. Though its forelegs seem to be raised in a devout attitude, the mantis is actually poised to pounce on its prey. Then, holding its victim in a grip of steel, it devours it at its leisure. Green or brown in color, this insect is about two inches long.

*How to Feed a Praying Mantis:* In captivity a mantis will usually accept bits of hamburger and other meat as substitutes for living prey. Mantids vary quite a bit in their eating habits; some are known to drink milk while others refuse it. They should be watered every day, and you can do this by sprinkling water on leaves in their cage. In time they may become tame enough to drink the water off a spoon.

During the winter, mantids' brownish egg cases, about the size of walnuts, may be collected from weeds and bushes. In the spring at least a couple of hundred babies will emerge from one of them.

*The Mantis as a Pest Exterminator:* The mantids of our southern states are native to this country, but one species found commonly in the more northerly regions originally came from China and Japan, while another is an import from Europe. Both were introduced here by accident; later more were imported for their supposed value in destroying insect pests. In China they are sometimes tied by a silk thread near a bedroom window where they trap flies and mosquitoes.

### WALKING STICKS—MASTERS OF CAMOUFLAGE

A youngster must be really sharp-eyed to discover one of these remarkably camouflaged insects. Aside from the fact that its coloring blends with the tree bark on which it so often rests, the walking stick has much the same shape as a slender twig. Unless it moves, you can scarcely tell it is an animal! In North America you will never see one flying, as all our species are wingless; but some of the tropical kinds have wings.

When a walking stick is detected and picked up, it is quite capable of playing dead—sometimes for several hours at a stretch. Though the largest American species is about six inches long, including the antennae, some found in India are known to reach a length of fifteen inches. Some walking sticks are able to grow a new leg, at least partially, to replace one lost through a mishap.

**WHICH IS THE WALKING STICK, WHICH IS THE TWIG?**

This aptly named insect is one of nature's most amazing examples of camouflage. Its color follows the seasons: green in springtime, brown in autumn to blend with the changing hues of the leaves. The walking stick can also play dead for several hours, if need be. It feeds on leaves, and is active mostly at night.

## The Misunderstood Spiders

Most of us think of the classic struggle between the spider and the fly as a war between two kinds of insects. But the spider is not an insect at all! Your youngster can discover this for himself if he watches one closely and counts its legs. The spider has eight legs—two more than an adult insect. Another distinction is that a spider has only two major body divisions—the head and thorax merged into one unit, and the abdomen—whereas an insect has three. Still another difference is that a spider, unlike an insect, has no antennae.

### THE SPIDER'S POISONOUS BITE

Spiders are widely misunderstood, much as snakes are. Many people believe that all spiders should be avoided or killed, that a spider bite is often fatal. In the United States we must beware of just two kinds: the tarantula and the black widow. Even in the case of these two species, the deadliness of the bite has been greatly exaggerated. If victims are properly treated, they recover promptly.

It used to be thought that black widows were found only in the South, but they are constantly being discovered—and always with great surprise—in New York, Connecticut, and other northern states. The large, hairy tarantula (the banana spider) also occasionally appears up north, after traveling as a stowaway in a bunch of bananas. In the tropics tarantulas are constantly on the prowl among this fruit for roaches and other insect food; so, chances are strong that a certain number will be moved aboard ship.

The bite of ordinary spiders is poisonous—that is the way they kill for food. Some bites cause swelling and irritation, possibly to the extent produced by a wasp's sting. However, the poison is usually administered in minute quantities; and few spiders are strong enough to be able to bite through a human skin even if they tried.

### STYLES IN SPIDER TRAPS

Spiders are past masters at keeping out of sight, but we have little trouble finding the silken traps they weave. Thus we rarely see the little house spider that prefers life indoors; still, we know it has been about when we discover cobwebs in dark and undisturbed corners. The funnel-shaped webs you may see spread over the fields if you go for an early-morning walk are the work of grass spiders.

A close relative of this species frequents cellars, so it is not surprising to find the same kind of funnel-shaped webs in your cellar. The most exquisite of all webs are those constructed by the orb builders, which often do their weaving in gardens or on porches.

*Remote-control Traps:* Sometimes you may find an orb weaver stationed at the center of its web, waiting for its prey; some species make a habit of this. Others, however, keep themselves hidden nearby. A spider that remains away from its web rests one of its claws on a trap line stretched from the hub of the web. When an insect enters the trap, the resulting vibration is carried to the spider, which rushes onto the web and envelops its victim in a band of silk. It bites the insect either before or after wrapping it, but usually does not eat it at once unless it is hungry.

*How the Spider Ingeniously Avoids its Own Trap:* A child may wonder, even if he has the opportunity to watch this drama being enacted, why the spider does not become entangled in its own web. He will understand why, if he knows that a web is made of two kinds of silk. One kind is inelastic and does not stick to objects that touch it; the other is very elastic and sticky.

The spokes of the web, the framework, and the guy-lines that fasten it to surrounding objects, are all of the inelastic silk. However, the continuous spiral lines connecting the spokes are very elastic and adhere to anything that touches them. The spider cleverly runs along the spokes and thereby avoids being tangled in its own web.

*How the Spider Spins an Orb Web:* If the spider is unlucky its web may be destroyed many times during a season. At times the little weaver may have to construct one every twenty-four hours. It begins its work on a well-elevated position by spinning a thread of silk which is soon caught in a passing breeze; the free end is carried along until it reaches an object to which it adheres. The spider then draws in the slack, making the line taut. It fastens the second end and walks across it, doubling its strength with another line of silk.

The spokes are constructed next, extending outward from a central point on this bridge line. Now the spider makes a spiral line a short distance out from the hub of these spokes and attached to each of them, holding them firm. The spider pulls this line tight, then continues weaving spiral lines until it reaches what will be the outer edge of the orb.

Up to this point all the silk has been smooth, tough, and not sticky. Now elastic, adhesive silk is manufactured as the spider makes a second series of spirals, this time working from the outer edge of the web down to the hub. During this process the spider cuts the first spirals with its jaws so that these lines fall away from the web. They have served their purpose as a mere scaffold! If you look very closely at a web, you may possibly see bits of the temporary spiral clinging to the spokes.

*Built-in Silk Spinner:* What the spider succeeds in spinning is so extraordinary that the result is quite certain to cause an observant child to wonder just how the silk is produced. This is the explanation: A spider has special spinning organs located near the top of its abdomen (in contrast to a caterpillar, which has its near the lower lip). There are two or three of these finger-like spinnerets, tipped with many small tubes. The silk is spun from them as a fluid but it hardens immediately upon coming in contact with the air.

*Spiders in Ambush:* Not all spiders construct webs; some kinds merely lie in wait for their prey. You may find white crab spiders doing this, though it is not easy to detect one of them. They are great artists at camouflage, taking on the color of the various flowers they hide in. Another spider that dispenses with a web is the trap-door spider, which makes a silk-lined home in the earth from which to stalk victims.

*How to Watch Spiders at Work:* You may occasionally succeed in moving an orb web with its weaver to your home, if it happens to be attached to a branch that you can break off conveniently. If you set it on a porch or some other likely place, you can then observe it at your convenience. However, it is more adventurous to watch spider traps being prepared in their natural setting.

You may have a chance to do this while you take an evening walk with your child; late in the day is the spider's usual time for spinning. You can even plot to have a web built as you look on. If you find one during the day with its builder lying in wait nearby, break it quietly and gently so as not to frighten the spider into running away. Then return to the scene during "building hours" and you should see a new web under construction.

### Spider Mothers Are Resourceful

Spiders have still another use for their silk. Eggs laid in the autumn to hatch in the spring need protection from weather as well as from hungry creatures. Many spiders solve this problem by spinning elaborate silken sacs for their eggs. Those that make cobwebs often suspend the sac from the web—or they may place the sac in a more sheltered spot. Others make nests for their eggs in folded leaves, or in the crevices of rocks and boards. Another custom is to nest on stones and cover the nest and eggs with a smooth, waterproof silken coat.

You may frequently see these little silvery disks as you walk through the fields in autumn. The large running spiders that you are most likely to find under stones not only make egg sacs—the mother attaches the sac to her spinnerets and carries it everywhere. When the young hatch, they climb on her back and stay with her for some time.

*Cannibal Spiders:* Even a mother's care cannot prevent her offspring from devouring each other. One of the common orb weavers, the orange garden spider, makes a very fine sac, about as large as a hickory nut, in which she may lay five hundred eggs or more. These hatch early in the winter but the young remain within the protective walls of the sac. By spring, when the sac breaks open, only a dozen or so young may emerge. They are the strong ones that have survived by consuming the rest of the once-large family.

### "Flying" Spiders

Possibly you have had the disconcerting experience of having a very tiny spider "fly" in your face on occasion. Particularly in the spring and autumn great numbers of these eight-legged creatures sail through the air and, especially to a youngster, it may seem they are actually flying.

However, if you look closely, you will see that the spiderling is attached to a long thread—still one more use for silk! Aided by the thread, it makes use of rising air currents to float from its hatching place to new territory, well apart from its numerous and hungry brothers and sisters.

*The Spider's Homemade Parachute:* To start its journey, the young spider climbs up a tall blade of grass or a larger plant. There it spins a silken thread and sends it out on the air. When it is long enough, the friction of air currents on it buoys it upward, and the spider, letting go its hold, is off on its journey to an unknown destination. Usually the flight is ended by the spider's bumping against an elevated object, but sometimes it helps decide its own fate by pulling in the streamer till all buoyancy is lost. "Flying" spiders have been discovered in mid-ocean!

Flying or ballooning is not the habit of just a few kinds of spiders. Most species use this means of getting from one area to another.

## Daddy Longlegs

If you observe the habits of this creature which, like the spider, is almost "all legs," you will find that it does not have the spider's ways. It does not spin silk, and it lays its eggs under stones or in crevices but gives them no other protection. Though it has eight legs and in many other ways resembles spiders, it is in an animal division of its own. We recognize it quite easily by its hairlike and remarkably long legs. If our legs were as long in proportion to our bodies as "daddy's" are to his, we would stand something like forty feet off the ground!

*"Tell Me Where the Cows Are":* Some children still learn the strange old custom of grasping a "daddy" and saying, "Tell me where the cows are, or I'll kill you." Its waving legs, as the little creature struggles to get away, are directed to all points of the compass, so that if there are some cows about, they are sure to be indicated. To a very young naturalist, this seems a satisfying experiment! But later he can learn facts about daddy longlegs that are much more interesting than this fanciful idea.

*How "Daddy" Uses His Long Legs:* This creature has the power of regrowing legs if they are broken off. The several pairs are of varying lengths: The first pair is usually the shortest, the second pair the longest and the fourth pair next in length. When you watch "daddy" running you can see that the second pair of legs are spread wide apart and keep in rapid motion. Their sensitive tips serve as feelers and relay information about the nature of the animal's surroundings. If they pause over something that suggests food, "daddy" stops running to investigate further with the little feelers (palpi) under its head.

*Observing Daddy Longlegs:* A daddy longlegs makes a most rewarding little captive. You can keep one for a while by simply putting a large glass tumbler over it. Place a few drops of sweetened water within convenient reach of the legs. It is amusing to watch this odd creature pull one leg at a time slowly through its jaws, nibbling it clean. A child can also see a little black dot on top of its body, located between the second pair of legs, which is apparently an eye! However, by examining it under a magnifying lens, he will discover that this is a raised knob, with a tiny shining black eye on either side of it!

## "Thousand-Leggers"

Children often call these creatures "bugs"—but they are neither bugs nor insects of any kind. They are in the same major grouping of the animal kingdom as insects, but each is recognized as a separate class in this division. This is quickly indicated by the fact that centipedes and millipedes have many pairs of legs—in contrast to the insects, which have three pairs of legs.

*More About "Thousand-Leggers":* Centipedes and millipedes have two main parts to their body structure: head and body. The millipede has two pairs of walking legs to each body segment, whereas the centipede has one pair to a segment. Their size and number of legs vary according to species, but all species of millipedes have so many legs that we frequently hear them called "thousand-leggers."

We usually find millipedes in damp places, though they may appear almost anywhere in a garden. They feed on vegetable matter and they do not bite. If they are disturbed, they roll up into a spiral.

The centipedes are not so harmless. They have a pair of poison fangs on the first segment of the flattened body. In northern regions centipedes are small and generally use their poison for killing insect prey. In tropical regions there are larger species of centipedes; their bite may have serious consequences for human victims.

## The Lowly Worms

Many a child who digs earthworms for fishing bait thinks he is collecting "insects." This idea is indeed very far from the truth. Worms are not closely related to any other creature; in the animal kingdom they occupy their own major niche, just as distinct as the division of "vertebrates" to which man belongs.

Scientists have classified the many kinds of worms in three main groups, and each of these forms one of the eleven major divisions of the animal kingdom. Some of our most troublesome parasites, such as tapeworms and hookworms, belong to two of these divisions—"roundworms" and "flatworms."

### How Earthworms Enrich the Soil

In the third group ("segmented worms") we find our friend the earthworm. "Friend" it is indeed, for earthworms are of immense value to man in growing food. As they move through the ground they do not push the earth around their bodies as a mole does; they actually swallow it! Before they expel the earth again, it is ground fine in the gizzard and lime is added to it in the stomach.

Earthworms usually plow a foot or more beneath the surface of the earth, and are constantly bringing subsoil upward. They also carry down with them from the surface bits of dead leaves, flowers, and twigs, which enrich the soil as they decay. Charles Darwin estimated that an acre of garden land in England held more than fifty thousand earthworms, and that eighteen tons of vegetable mold passed through each earthworm's body every year!

*Tug-of-War:* If a child watches a bird tugging at an earthworm, he may wonder what enables the worm to "hold on." The holding is done with strong muscles aided by tiny stiff bristles that cling to the earth. There are four pairs of bristles on each segment (or ring) of the worm's body, except for the first three segments and the last one. The bristles are aids in crawling as well as holding.

*The Earthworm's Eggs:* In the giant earthworms of the tropics which may grow to a length of six feet, it is easy to see how the body is composed of segments—one behind the other. On the common earthworm an extra, saclike ring is formed about the body toward its tail-end. The worm lays its eggs in this ring, and then works it forward and over its head. Cast off, the ring becomes a football-shaped capsule of yellowish brown, no larger than a grain of wheat. You may sometimes come across such a capsule in the fields, under stones or sticks, in May or June, before baby earthworms have hatched from the egg.

*Earthworms Are Profitable:* With the value of the earthworm fully recognized, raising worms has become a successful business enterprise. The earthworms are sold as fish bait to sportsmen throughout the United States and Canada—and, more important, they are supplied commercially to farmers who appreciate their ability to increase the fertility of the soil.

## The Insect World—Tiny or Immense

We have come to the end of our exploration of the enchanting world of insects, spiders, and other small creatures. It is a world tiny in scale but brimming over with fantastic, "wonder-full" things to observe: How insects see with their curious compound eyes, how they walk upside-down, walk backward, swim on their back, whirl in circles, make music, and change into gorgeous creatures through the magic of metamorphosis; how they make paper, produce honey, and weave silk; how they kill by piercing, sucking, trapping, entangling, or injecting nerve-killing fluid; how they build nests, combs, webs—or house themselves by fashioning a case over their bodies; how they live in huge colonies and fight in vast armies commanded by queens and served by slaves.